why teams don't work

why
teams
don't
work

·

what went
wrong and
how to make
it right

·

harvey robbins
and
michael finley

PETERSON'S/PACESETTER BOOKS
PRINCETON, NEW JERSEY

Visit Peterson's Education Center on the Internet (World Wide Web) at
http://www.petersons.com

Why Teams Don't Work is published by Peterson's/Pacesetter Books.

Pacesetter Books, Peterson's/Pacesetter Books, and the Pacesetter horse are
trademarks of Peterson's Guides, Inc.

Library of Congress Cataloging-in-Publication Data
Robbins, Harvey.
    Why teams don't work : what went wrong and how to make it right /
Harvey Robbins and Michael Finley.
        p.   cm.
    Includes index.
    ISBN 1-56079-704-5
    1. Work groups. 2. Work groups—United States. I. Finley, Michael,
1950-   . II. Title.
HD66.R583 1995
658.4'02—dc20   95-3270
                                                                   CIP

Cover and interior design by Kathy Kikkert

Printed in the United States of America

10 9 8 7 6 5 4 3 2 1

contents

acknowledgments • vii

introduction • 1

part one • broken dreams, broken teams

1 • The Team Idea—Everybody Get Together • 7

2 • Human Needs—Desperately Seeking Teaming • 17

3 • Individual Needs vs. Team Needs—Ulterior Motives • 21

4 • Teamwork vs. Socialwork—What a Team
We Would Make • 25

part two • why teams come apart

5 • Misplaced Goals, Confused Objectives—
What Are We Doing Here? • 29

6 • Unresolved Roles—It Ain't My Job, Man • 37

7 • Bad Decision Making—How Not to
Make Up Your Mind • 41

8 • The Wrong Policies and Procedures—
You Can't Get There from Here • 47

9 • The People Problem—I'm Not Working for That Jerk! • 51

part three • what keeps teams from working

10 • Leadership Failure—Who's in Charge Here, Anyway? • 75

11 • Faulty Vision—If You Don't Know Where
You're Going . . . You'll Probably Get There • 103

12 • Toxic Teaming Atmosphere—Organizational Karma • 107

13 • Communication Shortfalls—How'm I Doing? • 119

14 • Rewards and Recognition—Saying One Thing and
Doing Another • 129

15 • Depleted Trust—Why Should I Trust You? • 139

16 • Change Issues—Who's Rocking the Boat? • 153

part four • *team myths*

17 • The Myth of Adventure Learning—Belay That! • 171

18 • The Myth of Personality Type—It's What's Outside
That Counts! • 175

19 • The Myth That People Like Working Together—
Heigh Ho! • 179

20 • The Myth That Teamwork Is More Productive than Individual
Work—The Team! The Team! • 181

21 • The Myth of "The More, the Merrier" on Teams—
Let's Do 'The Wave'! • 183

part five • *turning teams around*

22 • Moving Teams Through Stages Toward Success—The Teaming
Goes Round and Round • 187

23 • Teams and Technology—The 24-Hour
Transworld Team • 201

24 • Long-Term Team Health—The Well-Tuned
First-String Team • 211

25 • Epilogue • 219

index • *223*

acknowledgments

We wish to thank all the great professionals at Peterson's Pacesetter Books, who encouraged us to create the "first second-generation book about teams." Specifically, this means our editor Andrea Pedolsky, with whom we brainstormed for four hours just to come up with the *name* for this book, and who rebuilt our fragile egos with every phone conversation. Andrea has been the third member of our team. It also includes, but is not limited to, Martha Kemplin, Bernadette Boylan, and Gary Rozmierski.

Harvey wants to thank all the teams he has worked with at all his client sites over the years, at Honeywell, 3M, Toro Co., IDS, CHQ, and other organizations. The people he met and worked with there are the heroes of this book, the team pioneers who taught us much with the hard lessons they had to learn.

Mike wants to acknowledge The Masters Forum, the Twin Cities executive education program that he has collaborated with, interviewing many of the speakers and authors that have visited and made presentations. Hearing them every month has been the MBA Mike always wanted. Much of the wisdom Mike contributed to this book is the reconstituted thoughts of these fine teachers.

And we both want to thank Nancy and Rachel, our real-life teammates, for putting up with the late-night work sessions and columns of looseleaf manuscript piled on every tabletop. We should probably thank one another's spouses, too, for the generous loan of their husbands. Thanks, Nancy. Thanks, Rachel.

Also the Highland Grill in St. Paul, which was the scene of many great working breakfasts, and whose hash browns are to die for.

introduction

Between us two co-authors, we have been describing this project to one another as "the first second-generation book about teams."

What does that mean? It means that there have been several good books written in the past decade about the promise of teams. Throughout the world, organizations have been trying to make this promise—of greater efficiency, greater flexibility, and greater productivity—come true.

But the reality has been falling short of the promise. The dream team, the first generation of team books described, seems beyond the grasp of most companies. Was the promise just a bunch of happy talk, or are there steps companies can take to make teams work better?

This book answers that question. Yes, there were a few slices of well-intentioned baloney in those books. But more important, there are indeed things managers, supervisors, and team leaders can do to give sputtering teams a tune-up.

This is a practical book. We have packed it full of down-to-earth questions and answers about teams, the obstacles preventing them from achieving their potential, and how to remove these obstacles. But there is also a persistent philosophical kernel embedded in these pages.

It is the simple, surprising, optimistic thesis that people want to work effectively together. Most of us positively ache to be team players.

Why is this surprising? Look around, to the left and to the right—people are not working together well. Teams are confused, misguided, ignorant, and often quite angry. People are not achieving even their median potential. Leaders are failing to lead. Organizations themselves, pyramids of weak teams, are vulnerable shells. The "dream team" is nowhere to be seen; that sleek machine of perfect clarity and execution is light years from the people we work with.

The dream team is up there in six-sigma-land—no more than a miscue or two per millennium. Virtually variation-free. Whereas, we here on the ground are variable like nobody's business. It's human nature. After all these centuries of jostling against one another, squinting, and misunderstanding virtually everything everyone says to us, we ought to have figured out that we are all different and understand things differently, and therefore we are continually miscommunicating.

But we don't. It's crazy, yet we have a natural inclination to assume otherwise, that we all share the same values and our team will automatically agree about all things. But values clash. Styles collide. And communication goes down in flames.

The ideal team, the one the first generation team books rhapsodized about, is a miracle of autonomous, cross-functional efficiency. It shares knowledge and creates solutions. It cuts costs. It's closer to the customer than paint.

Compared to that superteam, our teams are a bedraggled lot, rat packs and dirty dozens. Leaderless. Motionless. Clueless. Ten years after The Team took on the trappings of business fashion, thousands of organizations would like to give up on the idea—if they could.

This book seeks to supply team members and team leaders with tools and insights to get downtrodden teams back on track, talking to one another, and excited again about their missions. It is not rocket science. (When it comes to teams, not even rocket science is rocket science—teams at Cape Canaveral tie themselves in the same sailor knots that teams in your organization do.) Most any team can turn itself around simply by identifying what is hanging it up, and unhanging itself.

We thought of titling the book *Get Back*. Get back to the original optimism and willingness to cooperate that nearly everyone possesses—and undo all the clutter and confusion that gets put in the way of team success—that teams themselves often put there. Getting back is a simple concept, but it will take work, and lots of focus. We need to unlearn a ton of bad habits, assumptions, policies, and procedures.

A few of us won't make it. They have too much invested in the way things are, or they will just not be able to make the transformation. But those who are up for the challenge of the long haul, strap yourselves in. With a little assessment and the willingness to face the hard human facts, your team can pick itself up, dust itself off, and climb back on the horse.

part one

·

broken dreams, broken teams

chapter 1

•

the team idea

•

everybody get together

Ten years ago people didn't talk about teams. They existed, but they were conventional, function-bound things—accounting, finance, production, advertising teams, all made up of specialists in those functions or "silos." But a team revolution has occurred since then. The conventional silo team is still out there, but it has been crowded out by scores of other kinds of teams.

The world is teeming with teams. Work teams, project teams, customer support teams, supplier teams, design teams, planning teams, quality teams. Functional teams, and cross-functional teams. Committees, task forces, steering groups. Flat teams and hierarchical teams. Advisory teams and action teams. Teams with a structure and a charter, and teams that come together on an ad-hoc basis, do something, and fade back into the woodwork. Senior-level teams and rank-and-file teams. Leader-led teams and leader-less teams. Teams that live together and teams that never set eyes on one another. Teams as small as two or even one, and teams as unthinkably big as 20,000 people.

There are lots of kinds of teams, and each kind has its own unique potential to fall on its face.

The very word *team*, once as gritty and workaday as a word could be, has taken on attractive connotations:

- Magazine covers celebrate astute management and investment teams.
- Professional sports teams are selling for 20, 40, even 60 times book value.
- Dream Teams I and II, made up of the top professional players in the National Basketball Association, beat up on their Olympic counterparts from Uruguay, Lichtenstein, and Papua New Guinea.
- Think of the successful TV shows that have been about teams. *Star Trek, Charlie's Angels, The A Team.* The charm of many sitcoms was the mix of personalities on the workteam—*Mary Tyler Moore, Murphy Brown, The Untouchables.*
- Then there is that wonderful team series, *Mission Impossible.* They were the ultimate cross-functional team—diverse, brilliant, self-directed, good-lookin', and they had a terrific theme song.

So why does the whole world suddenly seem made up of teams? In the long course of history, teams have been the normal way of doing things. They have been a key component of organizational reality as long as there have been organizations. In the days of Hammurabi, teams were already old hat.

A family farm or a hardware store or a sawmill or school or an army platoon had to be operated by a team. Someone was usually designated the leader, and everyone else was assigned tasks according to their abilities. For a hundred thousand years, the world operated on a team basis. The team is the natural unit for small-scale human activity.

The catch, of course, is that word "small-scale." With the Industrial Revolution that began in the 1700s and that has taken the planet by storm, the common model for many businesses drastically changed. Mass assembly machinery and techniques developed in the early 1900s meant that a single man, woman, or even child in a factory could be ten times as productive as his or her cottage equivalent, working the old way.

The Industrial Age reached its apex with the development of scientific management. This theory, propounded by Frederick Taylor, an American, attempted to optimize the productivity of organizations by assigning minute tasks to individual members. Bosses were bosses. Below them were ranks of managers. Below them were countless supervisors. And below them, at the bottom of the organizational pyramid, were the multitudes of rank-and-filers, each one assigned a single, simple task, such as tightening a screw or attaching a hose or stamping a document.

Scientific management was the approach that yielded the phrase "a cog in the works." It was, in many ways, the wonder of the world. Henry Ford's River Rouge plant in Detroit was an impressive, four-mile-long monument to scientific management. The United States government was just as impressive. Its immense federal bureaucracy was also a form of scientific management. It broke a large organization down into a nearly infinite assortment of tasks. The hierarchy was very steep and very deep, from the clerk sorting applications in the U.S. Patent Office all the way up to his or her ultimate boss, the President of the United States.

Bureaucracy and the assembly line were technology-driven stages in organizational evolution. Machines allowed companies to do more, and people were brought in to "do the doing." The people hired at the base of the pyramid were generally uneducated factory workers, immigrants, or farm workers who had been driven off the land by technological advances there—the reaper, combine, steam plow, etc. Working for 30 cents an hour seemed like a good deal for the simple task of tightening a 9/16-inch bolt 2¾ turns clockwise, over and over and over.

Technology ratcheted the machine age even tighter with the development of commercial mainframe computers in the 1950s. Large companies were suddenly able to perform accounting chores—billing, buying, cataloguing, payroll, etc.—that were unthinkable even in the big-company boom of the 1920s.

Bolstered by the heavy iron of Univac and IBM, big companies became megacompanies. The emphasis began a subtle shift away from uneducated manufacturing crews toward well-educated professional functional groups—people skilled in engineering, finance, distribution, and even technology itself.

One look at a big company in the 1960s would tell you all you needed to know about the evolution of teams. In big companies they were nearly extinct, except as groups of professionals bound by functional skills—accounting teams, design teams, and information services teams.

Then, of course, the American postwar prosperity bubble popped. Corporations had become so immense that they were utterly out of touch with their customers. Workers were not asked to contribute their knowledge to the task of increasing an organization's ability to compete or make a profit. A deep trench separated management from workers; management was the brains of an operation, and workers were the muscle, and that was all.

Labor relations had become one of two things, each as bad as the other—adversarial to the point of intracompany war or complacent to the point of indifference. The driving mission of adversarial companies like U.S. Steel seemed to be to keep workers down. The sloppy mission of complacent companies like General Motors was to work with labor to make more big, profitable cars. Management and labor mopped up the gravy, and the customer was nowhere in the picture.

The world, which at the end of World War II was in ruins, was suddenly rebuilt, and fiercely competitive. Japan, Germany, and other countries were experimenting with new models for large organizations. Their successes at our expense were our wake-up call. The American engine of prosperity—huge factories, reductionist use of labor, vertical integration, and mainframe information control—was officially out of gas.

The new engine would turn the old pyramid on its head and would restore the focus to the forgotten, basic unit of operations—the workgroup or team.

What is a team?

A team is easily defined. It is *people doing something together.* It could be a hockey team making a power play; a research team unraveling an intellectual riddle; a rescue team pulling a child from a burning building; or a family making a life for itself.

The *something* that a team does isn't what makes it a team; the *together* part is.

Japan came at America in large part because of their team ethic. In the wake of the war they had no enviable natural resources, no state-of-the-art infrastructure, no money, no computers. What they had was motivated people with a cultural disposition to work together and the vision and patience to chart a strategy and see it through.

These people, working largely in teams, proceeded to clean our clock. Through the 1970s word wafted across the Pacific Ocean of the new approach the Japanese were using. Instead of asking the least from workers—tightening that 9/16-inch bolt 2 3/4 turns clockwise, over and over and over—the Japanese were asking the most. Every worker, in every function, at every level, was made a part of the company team. And that team's mission was the continuous improvement of processes. No idea was too small, and no worker was too small. Everyone participated.

Wm. Edwards Deming, the American statistician who helped get industrial Japan back on its feet in the 1950s, contributed some of the key concepts to the Japanese idea of continuous improvement or *kaizen*. Foremost among these was the notion that people, even people working on the shop floor or in the fields picking tomatoes, were human beings. Years after he returned to the U.S., having received Japan's highest honors, an acquaintance of ours asked him what the Japanese had taught *him*. Deming did not even look up from his dinner to reply. "People are important," he said.

Why teams are good

The reasons why organizations have been turning to teams have been put forward many times before and in several places. To sum up these advantages:

✔ *Teams increase productivity.* Teams are not excluded from the business thinking of the enterprise they are part of. As participants, closer to the action and closer to the customer, they can see opportunities for improving efficiencies that conventional management will overlook. Organizations looking to teams solely as a cost-reduction strategy have not been disappointed.

✔ *Teams improve communication.* In a proper team, members are stakeholders in their own success. Teams intensify focus on the task at hand. The business of a team is the sharing of information and the delegation of work.

✔ *Teams do work that ordinary groups can't do.* When a task is multifunctional in nature, no single person or crew of functionaries can compete with a team of versatile members. There is just too much to know for one person or one discipline to know it all.

✔ *Teams make better use of resources.* Teams are a way for an organization to focus its most important resource, its brainpower, directly on problems. The team is the Just-In-Time idea applied to organizational structure—the principle that nothing may be wasted.

✔ *Teams are more creative and more efficient at solving problems.* Teams are better for a host of reasons: they are motivated, they are closer to the customer, and they combine multiple perspectives. Result: they invariably know more about the length, depth, and breadth of an organization than a pyramid hierarchy can.

✔ *Teams mean higher-quality decisions.* Good leadership comes from good knowledge. The essence of the team idea is shared knowledge—and its immediate conversion to shared leadership.

✔ *Teams mean better quality goods and services.* The quality circle was an early expression of the idea that quality improvement requires everyone's best ideas and energies. Teams increase knowledge, and knowledge applied at the right moment is the key to continuous improvement.

✔ *Teams mean improved processes.* Processes occur across functions. Only a team that straddles all the functions contributing to a process can see what is happening and design ways to remove obstacles, speed up cycles, and apply organizational muscle where it matters most to the customer.

✔ *Teams differentiate while they integrate.* That sentence could use a little explaining. Organizations today want to downsize and work more effectively—but worry about the fragmentation that occurs with most downsizing. Teams allow organizations to blend people with different kinds of knowledge together without these differences rupturing the fabric of the organization.

This list reads like something taken from the team bible. The fact is that many, many organizations have been switching over—at least in their own minds—from the old pyramid hierarchy to the team ideal, and *they have not been experiencing the organizational bliss they counted on.*

They have tried teams, and they have seen teams stumble at the gate. Yes, the company saved money by eliminating or combining jobs deemed unnecessary—productivity by attrition. But communication, quality, and true productivity gains remain elusive. And now these companies are wondering: Was the team idea just another frantic—albeit protracted—business fashion? Is it time to hitch up the harnesses and rebuild the pyramid of bureaucracy?

The answer is that there is no choice except to plunge deeper into the team experience. The old way was simply too expensive. Any company tempted to turn back knows that it means taking on the waste and cost of old-line organizations that contributed to the competitiveness calamity in the first place.

The answer, rather, is to learn why teams have not been working out, and to change our organizations and our expectations, so that teams can achieve their considerable potential.

Where teams went wrong

Let's return to our history lesson. Last thing we knew, teams were being hailed as the greatest thing since beltless pants. At this point a fork appeared in the road. Companies came to it and, depending on their corporate cultures, veered to the right or to the left.

The two directions have been engagingly summed up by global strategist Gary Hamel, who says there are two basic corporate "orientations." These orientations correspond to the numbers above and below the line in any fraction:

Why Teams Don't Work
There is no single reason

PROBLEM	SYMPTOM	SOLUTION
Mismatched Needs	People with private agendas working at cross-purposes	Get hidden agendas on the table by asking what people want, personally, from teaming
Confused Goals, Cluttered Objectives	People don't know what they're supposed to do, or it makes no sense	Clarify the reason the team exists; define its purpose and expected outcomes
Unresolved Roles	Team members are uncertain what their job is	Inform team members what is expected of them
Bad Decision Making	Teams may be making the right decisions, but the wrong way	Choose a decision making approach appropriate to each decision
Bad Policies, Stupid Procedures	Team is at the mercy of an employee handbook from hell	Throw away the book and start making sense
Personality Conflicts	Team members do not get along	Learn what team members expect and want from one another, what they prefer, how they differ, start valuing and using differences
Bad Leadership	Leadership is tentative, inconsistent, or stupid	The leader must learn to serve the team and keep its vision alive or leave leadership to someone else

The top number, the numerator, is a company's potential for growth, expansion, core competencies, new products, new markets, generativity—profit by doing. The bottom number, the denominator, is the bottom line—cost containment, downsizing, flattening, delayering, dehiring—profit on paper.

Numerator companies have a vision of creating something terrific and new that didn't exist before. Denominator companies enlist in a more limited view, a zero-sum picture of mature markets that can never be expanded. Numerator companies came to the fork in the road and said, "Aha—we can use teams to leverage growth!"

Why Teams Don't Work

There is no single reason

PROBLEM	SYMPTOM	SOLUTION
Bleary Vision	Leadership has foisted a bill of goods on the team	Get a better vision or go away
Anti-Team Culture	The organization is not really committed to the idea of teams	Team for the right reasons or don't team at all; never force people onto a team
Insufficient Feedback and Information	Performance is not being measured; team members are groping in the dark	Create system of free flow of useful information to and from all team members
Ill-Conceived Reward Systems	People are being rewarded for the wrong things	Design rewards that make teams feel safe doing their job; reward teaming as well as individual behaviors
Lack of Team Trust	The team is not a team because members are unable to commit to it	Stop being untrustworthy, or disband or reform the team
Unwillingness to Change	The team knows what to do but will not do it	Find out what the blockage is; use dynamite or vaseline to clear it
The Wrong Tools	The team has been sent to do battle with a slingshot	Equip the team with the right tools for its tasks, or allow freedom to be creative

Denominator-oriented companies came to the same crossing and said, "Aha—we can use the idea of teams to trim the workforce!"[1]

If you see a good-guy/bad-guy fable developing here, you should probably disabuse yourself of the notion. Both numerator and denominator approaches are legitimate—indeed, all companies pursue both all the time, though they may tilt to one or the other. Cost-squeezing companies are not evil or mean-spirited. The approach is defensible in terms of the competition one is up against, in terms of the expectations of shareholders, and in terms of the personalities and experiences of top management.

---

[1] Gary Hamel and C. K. Prahalad, *Competing for the Future* (Cambridge: Harvard Business School Press), 1994.

Nevertheless, when they came to the fork in the road and chose to use teams primarily as a cost-cutting tactic, they set themselves up for a fall. No team thrives on being left to its own devices. A team is not a golden goose to be slaughtered for the single egg growing inside. It is not a money-saving "device." A team isn't any kind of device.

It is much more than that—it is a surprising, perplexing, up-and-down, tragicomic, value-creating human *thing*. A human thing that needs a ton of attention. That has to be pampered, fed, stroked, and have its pen hosed out from time to time.

Teams have the potential to do so much more than wring maximum value from a tightly held dollar. When they fail, it is often because the organization employing them took "the road most taken"—turning to teams to trim middle management, without giving the new teams the attention, tools, vision, rewards, or clarity that they need to succeed.

This book is about retracing a company's steps to that crucial cross-road and rethinking teams from the ground up.

Companies approaching teaming with the numerator or growth orientation do not write off the idea of bottom-line profitability. Far from it: there are incredible stories of growth at companies whose top managers have averted their gaze from the mechanical, baseline trance of achieving 9 percent return on investment ("Don't ask how we bring in the 9 percent, just do it!") and focused instead on team processes that are the seedbed for true market expansion.

Take care of team processes—eliminate waste and delay, streamline the workflow, consolidate handoffs, enlist the genius and enthusiasm of all your people, and hew to a powerful vision of meeting everyone's needs—and the bottom line has a crazy way of taking care of itself.

○○○

We have constructed the matrix "Why Teams Don't Work" on pages 14-15 to show how dysfunctional teams get that way. If your teams have all their pistons churning, you won't have a single problem in this matrix. More likely, your team is coming up short in one of the categories. Identifying the situation, and taking steps to understand and improve upon it, are what this book is all about.

chapter 2

•

human needs

•

desperately seeking teaming

The premise this book takes is that the human race is not a species of individual loners, each making our way by himself or herself, all alone in the world.

Nope. We are social creatures. We not only like one another's company, but we seek one another out in one situation after another. Deep down, we need this interaction, just as we need air, water, and life insurance.

Experts are not in perfect agreement about this. There seem to be a few of us who display a lot less need than the rest of us do. And some psychologists and anthropologists have indicated that there is also a dimension of the human psyche that does crave solitariness. Some people experience more of this than others.

What do we get from one another?

✔ *Affection.* People living without some kind of affection can scarcely be said to be living at all.

✔ *Affiliation.* The feeling of belonging to some kind of tribe, organization, or Moose Lodge.

✔ *Acknowledgment and recognition.* Who's to say a tree falling in the wilderness was ever there at all? Likewise, a life unacknowledged is a pretty thin thing.

✔ *Exchange of ideas.* The easiest and fastest way to learn is from other people. Without other people, the old wheel must be reinvented again and again and again.

✔ *Personal self-worth.* We see ourselves in terms of other people. Being social is at heart a process of personal benchmarking.

Truth is, despite that particle of us that craves isolation, our sense of ourselves withers without contact with others. This is not a platitude; it has been proven many times, throughout history. The process of denying someone access to others—isolation, banishment, banning, scapegoating—has been used for centuries in many cultures as a means of punishment. Primitive tribes declared a violator of tribal law a "nonperson." In England the practice of ignoring someone in disgrace was called "sending them to Coventry"; children were put "in Coventry"—a kind of extended "time out"—for being especially naughty. The Amish still practice a particularly nasty form of isolation called "shunning."

Disciplined societies like police forces, the military, and private schools have long histories of using the mental cruelty of isolation to deal with people who tattle on, sabotage, or otherwise undermine the group.

A more contemporary example is the explosion of computer networking. For decades, computer "nerds" have been isolating themselves in their fascination with technology. Today, suddenly, the isolation has come crashing down—the need for affiliation is a driving force behind the information superhighway. (It is a curiosity that two very profound organizational trends today cut directly against one another. Teaming forces workers together to a degree of intimacy they have not known before. The other trend, PC technology, has freed individuals from the need to team, and spawned telecommuting, bedroom businesses, and an army of autonomous consultants roaming the business landscape.)

Remember brainwashing? During the Korean War, it was discovered that you could make POWs believe anything you wanted—simply by cutting them off from interaction with other people. True-blue eagle scouts found themselves subscribing, in their lonely torment, to the politics of their jailers.

So, what has this to do with teams? The bright reader has guessed that what was true for the Akkadians in the 18th century B.C. is true for people today at AT&T. We still seek to affiliate with others. We still want them to like us. We still use one another to learn, to achieve complex tasks, and to enhance our individual value as contributors.

Banishment is still the punishment of choice at most organizations. We withhold information ("leave 'em out of the loop"). We isolate their jobs or their physical location ("our man in Murdo Bay"). We attack their credibility so no one is willing to work with them (the pariah syndrome).

Affiliation comes in different shades of intensity and happens for different reasons. Essentially, we affiliate in order to survive. The isolated individual is lonely; he is also ineffectual and short-lived.

The idea of teams and survival go hand in hand—it is a key theme of this book. For many team members, their team is their ticket to survival. It is quite literally their paycheck. The team provides strength of numbers ("They can't fire me—they'd have to fire the whole team.") and, often, foliage to hide their failures or averageness behind. These are the pluggers—unpretentious people eking out a living. They put their nose to the stone, and the other people at work, also with their noses to stones, are their team. They will do whatever they must, including team, to stay alive.

For other people, "stayin' alive" isn't enough. They need more than just subsistence, a job. They are on the lookout for a higher level of gratification, self-worth, the high of achievement. They want their little lights to shine, and they see their team as the way to do it. Survival-plus.

Work versus home is an issue. People getting their affiliation needs met at home—the marriage-as-team and the family-as-team—will often fall into the plugger camp at work. People not getting their affiliation needs met at home will see the workplace as the place to find this satisfaction. There are people so fulfilled by their role as team members that they wind up on scores of different teams, at work and in the community.

People not getting their affiliation needs met at either end may find themselves on a barstool somewhere, with an adopted team of affiliates, like Cliff Claven in *Cheers*. The barroom team is Claven's lifeline—take it away and you have one unfulfilled postman, and we all know where that can lead. (Mail-call!)

All we are saying is that people have a need to work with others. It does not begin to get at the problems that arise when people, drawn like mute, shiny-eyed, innocent primates to the idea of teaming, begin to drive one another crazy once they become teams.

As the bumper sticker says, bad stuff happens. Teams are put together wrong. They botch their assignments. They run aground because one lousy personality consistently wrecks their initiatives. They lack leadership, vision, motivation, a clue.

We'll get to the bad stuff in subsequent chapters. For now, try to empathize with the keen feeling that draws us together into teams in the first place.

Teaming isn't a newfangled idea, a fad, or an "initiative of the month." We have always teamed. It was the heart of early agriculture, 50,000 years ago. It was the heart, hundreds of thousands of years before that, of the hunt. Teaming is in our blood. We want to do it and do it well—but we have this tendency to muck it up in the execution.

When the going gets rough, it helps to remember that our intentions are good at heart, and very, very natural.

chapter 3

•

individual needs vs.
team needs

•

ulterior motives

People are born; teams are made. Both hurt like the dickens. Why? Because despite human beings' attraction to belonging to a team, we are not willing to uproot our individual lives and priorities for the sake of some lousy workgroup. So a conflict exists between individual team members' goals and the overarching goal of the team itself.

Let's illustrate that. A team of four has the goal of creating a lighter, longer lasting notebook computer battery for a computer company. Sounds simple. The four team members are: Stu, a designer; Diane, a tester; Eric, a manufacturing engineer; and Woody, a sales engineer.

That sounds workable. But the four people aren't stick figures.

The designer, Stu, has a chip on his shoulder because he feels he has already designed a battery that exceeds the specifications the team goal calls for. He feels demoted by being put on a team to do for the next six months what he spent the better part of last year doing. He is young and ambitious and would secretly like to start a company of his own and show everyone at the other computer companies what fools they are.

Diane, the tester, has been a part of teams too numerous to mention. Her professional goal would be to get some acknowledgment that her past contributions were key to the division's success. A single parent with three kids in their teens, she would like to give them more time, but she doesn't feel she can. Her dream is to take six months off and rest.

The manufacturing engineer, Eric, thinks he's God's gift to process management. His professional goal is to hit everyone over the head with a two by four and force them to utter the unutterable sentence: "Mind the processes and the results will take care of themselves." People are inclined to agree with that, but they wish he wasn't quite so smug about it all. Divorced, his kids all grown, he is all energy, a workaholic's workaholic. His individual goal is to prove that he is right and that everyone who has achieved more, risen to higher positions, and achieved greater recognition is a piker.

Woody, the sales engineer, is bright, young, and has a good track record for helping design technology that will sell. He felt two years ago that he was marked for higher things, but his career seems to have hit a wall. This team certainly cannot compare to the flat display team he helped run in 1993—they won product-of-the-year honors from several magazines. He dearly wants to score again like he did then—but he doubts this team, or its mission, has the gas to get him there.

We've just described four decent, talented people who are not in any way opposed to working on teams and have nothing major against one another. But there are numerous conflicts between their individual goals and the team goal, and these conflicts will only build in significance.

They probably won't ever blow up, or go ballistic, or meltdown into dysfunctionality. Nothing that dramatic. But they won't be a great team, and they won't meet their goal in a timely fashion, because their team goals are being subtly undermined by a raft of unfulfilled personal goals.

Stu, Diane, Eric, and Woody are not going to click. Not for lack of good intentions. But their good intentions, taken together, are a feeble force compared to their individual, unaddressed needs.

Rebalancing the load

Effective teamwork means a continual balancing act between meeting team needs and individual needs. We're not just talking about the basic human need for survival through affiliation with others that we discussed in the last chapter. We are speaking of all the things that each of us wants, things that have nothing to do with teams or jobs.

While it's nice to be around other folks and work with them, we are, all of us, still looking out for number one. Forget all the movie scenes of the scrappy doughboy jumping on a live grenade to save his buddies in uniform. In real life, we take actions with others primarily to satisfy our personal agendas. People will only agree to team if it meets their own needs first.

Of course, there are some of us who live for deferred gratification as a masochistic kick, like agreeing to work toward a team outcome now in exchange for some personal outcome later on. These people happily forestall today's druthers in order to incur team payback tomorrow.

But, in general, it's a "me first" or at least a "please consider my needs while we meet the team's" kind of world.

Find the agenda

"Good soldiers" are sometimes not soldiers at all. Teams must be leery of members who have no honest intention of being working members of the team. In their hearts, they are saying:

- "I'm not here to work with the team, but to take credit for its successes."
- "I'm not here to work with the team, but to associate with some of its members."
- "I'm not here to work with the team, but to use it as a steppingstone to better things."

The term "hidden agenda" was coined to describe this kind of covert careerism. It is not honest and it is very destructive to team coherence. Good teams recognize the fact that in order to build trust, they must uncover their own hidden agendas and expose them to the light of day.

Diane, Eric, and Woody must be made aware of Stu's misgivings and discontent. Stu, Eric, and Woody should understand that Diane's heart will not long be in her work if she is frustrated and exhausted and on the brink of despair. Eric's peculiarities must be conceded by the rest of the group and the intensity of them harnessed to push the group toward its own stated goal—and not undermine it. Woody's ambitions can be achieved much more readily if Diane, Eric, and Stu agree to succeed together and make the best battery the world ever saw.

Who is to say that the team mission is the only mission that a team can acknowledge and pursue? Deep down, most of us are not especially good soldiers, and we do not long to subordinate our own desires to the common good. Live grenades—alas—do not get leaped on routinely.

To the contrary: sacrifice, loyalty, and the willingness to go through a little hell for one another occur only when the cards are on the table and people are allowed (and required) to be honest about their needs.

Personal goals that prevent us from achieving team goals are often very honorable:

- having a baby
- spending more time with family
- seeking a better job after this one
- going back to school and getting that degree

Or they can be a shade less edifying:

- making a name for oneself
- joining a team that is clearly funded
- wanting to belong to a team of "winners" for a change
- wanting a group that one can dominate
- glomming onto a team that has already achieved successes
- hiding behind a powerful executive's support and championship

Whatever the personal goals, we need to know what they are, and to deal with them, or at least acknowledge them, as a team—perhaps even to make them corollary team goals. When we know what our fellow team members want us to achieve and what we ourselves want, that is a terrific bond between members.

The sooner we know one another's personal needs and hopes, the better for the team. This doesn't mean these personal needs have to be completely met first before true teaming can get under way. It does mean that acknowledging and addressing these needs as a group, early on, can help prevent our "selfish" desires from sinking the team effort.

chapter 4

•

teamwork vs. socialwork

•

what a team we would make

In the last chapter we talked about personal goals that interfere with team goals. This chapter adds another category of goals that we call "socialwork." These are sort of like team goals because they involve the group, but they aren't related to the business goals. Basically, they are fun stuff, distractions.

The stated purpose for a team is to gather people together and collaborate to jointly accomplish agreed upon team outcomes; i.e., get things done together. The purpose of socialwork, on the other hand, is to get your personal needs for affiliation met by being involved in a group.

One is work-related, the other not.

Here are examples of teamwork attractions that distract members from the true team goal:

- the team has some super attractive members
- the team has a charismatic leader
- the team gets to travel
- the team has an incredible expense account
- the team was written up in *Fortune*
- the team gets a great workspace

- the team does no lifting
- the team goes to Vail every February

This is a mixed list, but what it says is that there are more reasons for joining a team than just the human need to interact or the validity of the stated team goal ("develop a manned flight rocket to travel to the Sun"). Knowing these things about one another, up front, can resolve anxieties and expectations before they drag the team down.

Sometimes the line between teamwork and socialwork gets a bit fuzzy. You can usually tell this is happening when everyone on a team is pissed off. An example of the teamwork/socialwork clash is when Team Member A is working on a task while Team Members B, C, and D are in the next cubicle chatting away about nonwork-related things. While A is doing teamwork, B, C, and D are doing social work.

It is a uniquely human conflict—work vs. play. While play is natural and normal, it quickly becomes corrosive when play replaces work as the goal for one or more team members. It will not take long for Team Member A to resent the fun the others are having and their unwillingness to pull their share of the load.

Conversely, Members B, C, and D will feel genuinely indignant and angry that their socializing is not perceived as the vital glue that holds the team together. Hint: If glue isn't being attached to every team member, it isn't vital glue.

A survey a few years back suggested that during an average workday, at least one fourth of the time is occupied by socialwork. The researchers also suggested that this mental break time is a necessary component to staying sane at work (relieving stress). The problems occur when some people on a team are teaming at the same time others on the same team are socializing.

Some team members have higher needs at one end of the spectrum than the other. Some people never seem to need or want a break, while others don't appear to be pulling their weight since they're usually schmoozing. All work and no play makes you dull. All play and no work makes you unemployed. A coordinated balance makes you more productive. While both teamwork and socialwork are essential to team success, getting the whole team in sync is important.

part two

·

why
teams
come
apart

chapter 5

•

misplaced goals, confused objectives

•

what are we doing here?

We've heard colleagues say it just slightly fewer than a thousand times: "My boss sets such unrealistic expectations/goals/objectives/targets." They're really saying one of three things:

✔ *They don't believe in the outcome.* The boss is famous for her five-year plan. But no one has paid any real attention to it in, oh, five years.

✔ *They don't believe the outcome is reachable.* Maybe the boss is blowing blue smoke again, pulling figures out of a hat. Worse, maybe she read an article about "stretch goals" and has the bright idea of stretching us to meet the goals.

✔ *They can't figure out what the boss really wants as an outcome.* Teams fail when their reason for being is unclear. The goal is expressed complicatedly, ambiguously—in dollars, in eliminated defects, in market share, in new customers. How do you focus simultaneously on four focal points?

Whichever of the three it is, people are stuck in the blocks, unable to start the race.

If you don't know where you are going or what you want the outcome to be/look like, the only option left is prayer. Fall to your knees and beg the stampede to step lightly over you. Barring divine intervention, you'd better create a positive and compelling expectation of the outcome if you're ever going to muster the troops to collaborate.

Plus, actions toward outcomes don't happen in a vacuum. They must link up with other mobile bodies bouncing down the corridors toward their own outcomes. If they are not deliberately linked together, they will trip over one another. Failing to create realistic goals and linking them with others can be a fatal team error.

To understand the length, breadth, depth, and pH of the pickle such a team is in, you have to understand what a goal is.

Leaders, visions, goals

A goal is not a number. Wm. Edwards Deming, who knew more about human motivation than a boatload of organizational behaviorists, was very clear in his famous fourteen points that numerical targets and quotas do vastly more damage than they do good.

A proper goal takes advantage of what we have been discussing—the natural disposition of people to work together on teams. It begins with the vision of the leader that a task is desirable and performable. The leader may be a member of the team, may be a core within the team, may even function primarily outside the team. But he or she (or they) must have credibility within the team.

The vision is translated by credible leadership into a concrete aspiration. *Kennedy said, "We will put a man on the moon."* That sentence explains almost everything you need to know about leadership and goals. It is clear. It is significant. And it engages.

A leader whose goals are constantly shifting is no leader at all. A stated goal stabilizes and concentrates the vision of the leader into something that is clear and concise and represents a continuing vision of what the team hopes to achieve together. A good vision is an act of faith that a difficult, worthwhile goal can be achieved.

If the goal is clear enough and engages people's hearts as well as their minds, the goal itself assumes much of the burden of leadership. It becomes a continuing corrective against distraction, confusion, and decay.

Unless the team is a company's executive team, a team goal is not the same as a strategic goal. Strategic goals properly call for ambitious, broad, long-range achievement. Team goals usually have a more modest ring to them. If they don't, check to see that the team isn't biting off more than it can chew.

A good team goal has several parts:

- a *task*; what are you doing
- a promised *limit* of what you're doing; unlike the enchanted brooms in *The Sorceror's Apprentice*, you know when to stop
- a promised *level of performance*; you'll spare no expense; you'll stick to a tight budget; it will be world-class work; "good enough" is not good enough
- a *deadline*; a sunset clause, after which even the best coach reverts to the role of pumpkin
- the definition of the *customer*, who all this effort is for

Interteam warfare

Harvey recalls an experience from a few years back, at one of the larger and more prestigious bomb factories in our nation, back when we knew who the enemy was. Trouble was brewing because of a lack of linked goals. Not with our allies, but inside the factory.

The company had just won a contract for a very advanced weapons system. This weapon was so complicated, so sophisticated, so cutting-edge that making it required seven separate teams; each team working on a different part of this multi-tank killing mini-rocket, code-named Fluffy.

The potential of the system out on the battlefield was mindblowing. Equally mindblowing, however, were the conniption fits the seven teams experienced putting one together.

The problems began at the goal stage. Thrilled with the technological opportunity at hand, the seven teams neglected to link their goals together. Like a scavenger hunt, each team was instructed to pool its best ideas and meet at the end of a two-month idea-sharing progress meeting. As the date drew near there was a sense of excitement in the air; that morning the room was atingle with engineerial delight.

Each team got to report on its part of the project to date. The first team got up to speak and with great pride explained their innovative approach to opening the flaps covering the launch tube. As they spoke, there was a rumble from some of the other teams. One person stood up and yelled at the speaker, "You idiot, if you do that, your flaps will cover up our sights and we can't see what we're shooting at." Another team chair chimed in, "Our electronics array hasn't been designed to do that!" Etc., etc., etc.

Remarkably, the meeting went downhill from there. Recriminations, reprisals, faces slapped, duels arranged at dawn in the marshy area down by the bullet casings shed. Months of product development, time, and many millions of dollars were lost because of a lack of linked goals. It took two additional months for respective team members to overcome their anger and multidirectional finger pointing.

Team sadism

Another team excess to guard against is team sadism. There are various degrees of rigor you can expose your team to. On one end of the spectrum you can make life too cozy for your team. Peel their grapes, talcum their bottoms, etc. That's no good—teams thrive on a certain degree of anxiety.

The opposite extreme, however, can be horrific. We have known managers and team leaders who were nearly psychopathic in their willingness to cause team pain.

Take the phrase "stretch goal." It is a perfectly legitimate idea. It is simply an ambitious goal you set for organizational performance. Motorola's goal of Six Sigma errorlessness (limiting quality defects to 2 or 3 per million outputs) was a stretch goal. Difficult but, as Motorola has proven, achievable without massive bloodshed.

But there are boneheads out there who focus not on what is achievable but on how much it stretches the team. In their minds a stretch goal would be a fivefold increase in team productivity. It was painless for them to utter the goal at a team meeting, but oh, the pain it caused team members in the year that followed.

We knew a manager in Minnesota who joked about his motivational methodology. "I chase 'em up a ladder, then I kick it out from under 'em." Nice guy. It is one thing to throw your team in a tank to teach it to swim. Call it tough love. But it's something else to stock the tank with piranha, or to fill it with boiling oil.

The road to nowhere

Teams seeking to create trust and instill a sense of strong leadership must clearly define and then link their goals or objectives. This isn't a maybe, it's a you have to. After all, if you don't know where you're going, any road will take you there.

No two roads are alike, of course. When a team is assigned a task, it feels lucky to be placed in an orderly environment. It's nicer cruising down a four-lane highway than warily hacking a footpath through the jungle. But many assignments put teams squarely in the jungle—creating something from nothing; creating (and this is often worse) something from something; building bridges between different ideas, cultures, products, teams; cleaning up the messes previous teams made.

Work is often confusing, cluttered, and inconvenient. People are always people, with all the variation and inconsistency that humanity implies. Given the inherent disorder of most team tasks, teams simply must insist on diamond-like clarity at the onset of a mission, with a hard-edged understanding of the impending task.

Goal-setting by the spoonful

Goal-setting often fails because people get hung up on the long-term aspect of the primary goal. "Retake Granada" was an overarching goal that took Spain 500 years. It might have been achieved quicker had *El Grande Objecto* been broken down into component mini-goals from the start.

That is what proper goal-setting is—you start with a grand supergoal that the entire team is striving for, and then you chart a path toward achieving it, with team members assigned to a series of doable, short-term steps.

Successful teams live and breathe the short term. That is where the action is, and that is where intelligence is put to work. They may plan longer term, but they act for the present.

They also concentrate on a few goals at a time. New teams are famous for declaring 30 goals or outcomes when they first come together. There are some organizations that require the creation of a list of every action a person is to perform during the next performance cycle—maybe a year, maybe longer. This is what passes for long-term vision in many organizations.

The problem is that when confronted with a list of 20 to 30 objectives, the tendency of most sentient beings is to go into shock and do nothing for a period of recovery. The human brain is a dazzling organ, but not even people with brains in good working order can work on more than two objectives at the same time.

Goals that are not being worked on at the present tend to gnaw at one's mental innards. This decreases productivity. We may state this as a rule: the more goals and objectives a team is handed, the worse their performance will be.

Master plans to the contrary notwithstanding, things have a way of changing. Allow for flexibility as time passes, for the list of goals and objectives to be amended as new knowledge leads to new understanding. One of the horrors of organizations is seeing an individual confronted by a manager for the noncompletion of goals that anyone who has been paying attention knows are no longer relevant.

The long and the short of it

The short-term is where it's at. Not "Retake Granada," but "Start with that blue row-house on Seville Street, the one with white shutters."

Focusing on the doable allows a team to achieve instant, perfect understanding and to strike quickly, like commandos.

So what constitutes short?

We begin by proposing task durations much shorter than you may currently use as benchmarks. We sort all goals and objectives into short-, mid-, and long-term time frames. Short means less than one month (like next week); mid means 1 to 3 months; long-term means 3 to 6 months.

So much for the vaunted 100-year plan. But that is just the point anything beyond 6 months takes you into the realm of pipe dreaming and strategic planning. Too many things can go wrong, or change. One little bend in the river can wipe out months of work and devastate morale.

If you have a goal pushing beyond the 6-month limit, break it down into shorter term tasks that fit into these three time frames. That way the team is continuously knocking down fresh goals and objectives, experiencing successes, staying on track, moving quickly, and raising team motivation.

Commando teams are small, single-goal, and short-term. When their goal is accomplished, they disband back into the larger organization only to be regrouped again into other short-term action teams.

Once a team lists its goals and objectives and sorts them into the appropriate time frames, the team must then prioritize the short list. If a task doesn't appear on the high priority, short-term goals/objectives list, the hell with it. *Leave all the rest behind.*

As time passes and mid-term goals/objectives move into the short period, reprioritize the new short list. If the goals/objectives at the bottom of the priority list are still there when the team reprioritizes, then repeat what you did before—ignore them. Under no circumstances are you to complete these tasks. You are hereby forbidden even to worry about them—which you might well do without our strict instructions.

These unfulfilled pledges have a name, and that name tells you everything you need to know about them—*goal sludge*. They are not bad or evil, they are just not especially useful. They must either be delegated to others, who may give them a higher priority, or they can be left to die in the stinking desert sun.

The final element

One final element is critical to good goal-setting—passion.

The world is full of boring visions. Whole organizations drag themselves from quarterly report to quarterly report pursuing them. It is as if the leadership has read all the right books and has made up its mind not to make any obvious mistakes but neglected to make the goal interesting in any way.

A dull goal lacks originality, personality, sizzle. A good goal goes beyond setting a numerical target or quota. It goes beyond some lame mission statement language about becoming world-class, or best-in-breed, or worm-free, or whatever the fad phrase in the consulting community is this week.

Because people want to be turned on by their work. A good goal gives them something to respond to. Something to buy into and claim ownership over.

chapter 6

•

unresolved roles

•

it ain't my job, man

When we were kids, we didn't worry about roles and responsibilities. We swarmed through the neighborhood, doing what we pleased, or what we were told until we got distracted and did something else. We were an army without ranks, a tribe of generalists, a corporation without job titles—a nonhierarchical, de-layered, super-flattened, inverted-pyramid, matrix/cluster mob. And we liked it.

Fast-forward to the pre-team era, and the workplace was lousy with roles. Every worker had a job description. Every job description described exactly what workers' tasks, roles, and working relationships were. Both, as a rule, were defined quite narrowly—second-level lab technician, plastics, assistant to first-level lab technician, plastics.

In today's team era, job descriptions have become less precise, broader, and roles are hardly mentioned on paper. But these roles and relationships, whether committed to print or not, themselves play important roles in successful teaming.

The idea of teams is that people are adults. We're too grown up for the pigeonholing of conventional job descriptions and scientific management. But many teams, in their new freedom, have reverted to swarming through the neighborhood. They are doing what they want to do, or what they are good at. Important but less desirable work often is not getting done.

Somehow, team members have to have three conditions in effect:

1. all members must know the task they must complete . . .

2. without those roles and responsibilities becoming straightjackets and cutting off circulation to the brain . . .

3. while making sure that all necessary work gets done, including the scutwork, which thinking people hate. . . .

It is a tall and a paradoxical order.

Hot potatoes

There are tasks out there that no one wants to do. They are routine, or unpleasant, or they do not play to our strengths. Paperwork is probably the number one item to avoid. Phone calls bother some people. Evaluating people. Filing reports. Getting rid of the old grounds in the coffee pot. Terrible things. But—they still have to be done. The trouble occurs when team members refuse to handle these hot potatoes.

There are many variations on this theme. People refuse tasks for different reasons. Their excuses are good ones:

- "I'm no good at that."
- "I did it last year."
- "Don't you remember what happened the last time I did that?"
- "If you make me do that, we won't be friends anymore."

Managers and team leaders bend over backward to find some way to get these tasks done without forcing team members to do them. They pass them on to resource team members or farm them out completely to third-party providers. Or they, too, turn their back on the unpleasant tasks and ignore the mounting negatives.

Harvey once overheard a seasoned professional having a woodshed talk with a raw recruit about what makes up a good team member. He was saying, "Ya know, Jake, sometimes ya just gotta suck it up and do things ya don't like."

No one wants to hear that, but it's true. Everyone on a team must pull their fair share of scutwork if the team is to succeed. Exempt some team members but require it of the others, and you have a two-tier team, which is a no-no. The scutwork in any organization tends to go undone except by a few people looking for martyr points. These orphaned tasks, roles, responsibilities pile up and, after a while, start screaming for attention. The emergency nature of these screams takes a team off its measured plan and forces them to stamp out the fire.

Like the auto oil filter commercials used to say, "Pay me now, or pay me later." Let unpleasant tasks go unassigned, and thus undone, and you will learn the true meaning of unpleasant.

Turf wars

Problems also occur when more than one person on a team has responsibility for a single (usually appealing) task. A classic example of this is the senior management team that is not a team at all, because the ambitions of individual members are superseding the team mission. The result: turf wars. Both parties perceive a task as their turf and are prepared to violate the spirit of collaboration to ensure the turf remains theirs.

People will fight over just about anything, if they are convinced the turf in question represents power for them, or if they perceive they are painted into a corner: members of a public relations firm fighting one another to maintain control of an account; co-leaders of a workteam doing battle over who keeps the books or has access to the team sponsor; members of an otherwise purely collaborative effort coming to blows over whose name appears first on the final report.

∘O∘

Both hot potatoes and turf wars spell disaster for team success. Effective teams recognize these potentials, plan for them, and communicate more often when confronted with them.

In the case of hot potatoes, rotating the scutwork through all team members (even the most senior) sends a clear message of "pulling your team load." On this team, *everyone* does the dishes. Be careful, however: perhaps no one wants to take on the hot potato because no one is really qualified to do the task—bookkeeping, say. When there is a genuine gap in team talent, you have to recruit someone else to do the work, if only on a short-term basis.

When turf wars occur, openly negotiate specific tasks. How you communicate content, and how you agree on procedures for updating, linking, collaborating, and accountability are crucial.

Remind people that great teams are cross-functional in design. As in war, team members back one another up. Cross-trained people have primary and secondary roles. If one person goes down (with another task, or with the flu), another team member steps forward and fills in.

Remember to ask this critical question periodically:

Who's responsible for what, by when,
and how are we going to check with each other
to make sure we're still on track?

chapter 7

.

bad decision making

.

how not to make up your mind

There was a time in his life, back around 1970, when Mike worked as an autoclave technician at a large metropolitan hospital. Though he worked the graveyard shift, he was still astonished at the military orderliness of the sterile laboratory's work regimen. The shift supervisor watched everything like a hawk and clocked every tray that went in or out. She and she alone filled out all requisition forms. She kept these forms on a clipboard, which she passed on at sunrise to the day shift officer, er, manager replacing her. Not only was Mike not allowed to make decisions, *she* wasn't allowed to. It was strict.

One night, when the supervisor was on break, a nurse came dashing down the hall, in urgent need of a scrub set for some procedure. Mike swallowed hard and handed it to her, without filling out the usual paperwork. The next day he was fired for allowing supplies to leave the area without paperwork. He had to turn in his Foley clamps and surgical mask. It was all very sad. But Mike was philosophical—at least some motorcyle accident victim up in the ER got the asphalt cleaned out of his wound.

This was a case of too-tight central control causing the team to fail in its stated mission of helping patients. The way a team decides to decide is one of the most important decisions it makes. You may want to read this last sentence again. It is not a misprint.

Teams start by learning, and they hit their stride when they act. How action is triggered varies according to the action in question. Right decisions are decided the right way. And vice versa: Napoleon's choice to duke it out with Wellington at Waterloo was not just a bad decision; it was the battle.

What's even more dangerous in the long term is consistently relying on the wrong process to arrive at decisions. How did Napoleon decide to head into the trap awaiting him on the Flemish plains? He just decided, all by himself, that's how. It was the Napoleonic way.

Perhaps if he had shown a bit of executive flexibility and followed another method of decision making, he and his team in arms might have had a better day on the field. He had seven options, each one suitable for a specific kind of situation. Napoleon, being an autocrat, would only have been amenable to a couple of the decision-making approaches. Your team, over the weeks and months of working together, may have to use them all:

☞ **CONSENSUS.** Consensus decision making is where all team members get a chance to air their opinions and must ultimately agree on the outcome. If any team member does not agree, discussions continue. Compromise must be used so that every team member can agree with and commit to the outcome.

Advantages: Produces an innovative, creative, high-quality decision; elicits commitment by all members to implement the decision; uses the resources of all members; the future decision-making ability of the team is enhanced; useful in making serious, important, and complex decisions to which all members will be committed.

Disadvantage: Takes a lot of time and psychological energy and a high level of member skill. Time pressure must be minimal. There can be no emergency in progress. Bring pajamas—you could be doing this all night.

☞ **MAJORITY.** Majority decision making is democracy in action. The team votes, majority wins. Simple.

Advantages: Can be used when there's no time for a full-dress consensus decision, or when the decision is not so important that consensus is necessary, and when 100 percent member commitment is critical for implementing the decision; closes discussion on issues that are not highly important for the team.

Disadvantages: Usually leaves an alienated minority, a time bomb for future team effectiveness; important talents of minority team members may be snubbed; commitment for implementing the decision is only partially present; full benefit of team interaction does not happen.

☑ **MINORITY.** Minority decision making usually takes the form of a subcommittee of a larger team that investigates information and makes recommendations for action.

Advantages: Can be used when not everyone can get together to make a decision; when the team is in a time crunch and must delegate responsibility to a committee; when only a few members have relevant expertise or knowledge; when broader team commitment is not needed to implement the decision; useful for simple, routine decisions.

Disadvantage: Does not utilize the talents of all team members; does not build broad commitment for implementing the decision; unresolved conflict and controversy may damage future team effectiveness; not much benefit from team interaction.

☑ **AVERAGING.** Averaging is the epitome of compromise; it is how our esteemed Congress decides: team members haggle, bargain, cajole, and negotiate an intentional middle position. Usually no one is happy with the result except the moderates on the team.

Advantages: Individual errors and extreme opinions tend to cancel each other out, making this a better method than "authority rule without discussion."

Disadvantage: Opinions of the least knowledgeable members may annul the opinions of the most knowledgeable members. Little team involvement in the decision making, so commitment to the decision will likely be weak. Letting members with the greatest expertise make the decision is almost always better than a group average.

☛ **EXPERT.** This is simple. Find or hire experts, listen to what they say, and follow their recommendations.

Advantages: Useful when the expertise of one person is so far superior to all other team members that little is to be gained by discussion; should be used when the need for membership action in implementing the decision is slight.

Disadvantages: How do you determine who the best expert is? No commitment is built for implementing the decision; advantages of team interaction are lost; resentment and disagreement may result in sabotage and deterioration of team effectiveness; knowledge and skills of other team members are not used.

☛ **AUTHORITY RULE WITHOUT DISCUSSION.** This is where there is usually no room for discussion; like predetermined decisions handed down from higher authority. Moses on Mt. Sinai. Trust is often killed with this method when a team leader tries to fool team members into thinking that their opinions about the decision really can affect the decision. Team members know when a team leader is jerking them around.

Advantages: Applies more to administrative needs, useful for simple, routine decisions; should be used when very little time is available to make the decision; when team members expect the designated leader to make the decision; and when team members lack the skills or information to make the decision anyway.

Disadvantages: One person can not be a good resource for every decision; advantages of team interaction are lost; zero team commitment is developed for implementing the decision; resentment and disagreement may result in sabotage and deterioration of team effectiveness; resources of other team members are not used.

☛ **AUTHORITY RULE WITH DISCUSSION.** This method is also known as Participative Decision Making. Unfortunately, most people don't know what this really means. Many leaders think that they have to give up their decision making responsibility. There is nothing further from the truth. Under this method, those in the decision making role make it clear from the onset that the task of decision making is theirs. Then they join in a lively discussion of the issues; their opinions count just like other team members. When they have heard enough to make an educated decision, they cut off the discussion, make the decision, then get back to all team members to let them know how their inputs affected their decision. Most team members feel listened to and are willing to participate in another team decision using this method.

Advantages: Gains commitment from all team members. Develops a lively discussion on the issues using the skills and knowledge of all team members. Is clear on who is ultimately accountable for the decision of the team.

Disadvantages: Requires good communication skills on the part of team members; requires a leader willing to make decisions.

○○○

Though fashion occasionally underscores one or another of these approaches, there is no right or wrong way to decide an issue. The important thing is that *the team decide, in advance, what decision making method will be used.* No surprises. If members are apprised of the process, even autocratic methods acquire the consent and blessing of all.

chapter 8

•

the wrong policies and procedures

•

you can't get there from here

One of the responsibilities Harvey had, as a rookie psychologist working for the government, was writing policies and procedures manuals (P&Ps) for groups out in the field. Ninety-nine times out of 100, his group wrote serious, sober, usable policy books. Every full moon, however, they succumbed to the impulse to create a manual of complete gibberish, full of elliptical provisions that no team in their right mind would follow—mad, foolish, twisted, bureaucratic stuff. And, figuring no one read the books anyway, they sent them out.

Imagine their horror to discover, on field trips many months later, that these policy and procedure manuals were being treated as though they had been handed down on Mt. Sinai on stone tablets. People actually went out of their way to try and make the absurd nostrums work, wasting time and productivity along the way.

Harvey was not only ashamed that he had had a hand in contributing to the delinquency of our government, but he was angry at the lemmings who blindly followed the obviously idiotic policies he had scripted.

What we have learned

The lesson of this shameful episode—Harvey still bursts into tears at odd intervals, just thinking about it—is that some balance has to be found in the area of policies and procedures. On the one hand, organizations and teams themselves must create policies and procedures that are credible. Credibility means that the information in the P&Ps must parallel reality.

Too many companies and too many teams live a double life—their life by the book and their real life. When the book and reality diverge too sharply, they acquire separate lives. People who perform well in the actual organization go with the flow of the organization; people who perform better "by the book" will cling to it, chapter and verse, stifling their own growth and creativity.

Those who snicker at policies and procedures manuals are really snickering at their corporate culture. They are acknowledging that their organization, and they themselves, are living a lie. Bad rules have a corrosive effect on the bond holding teams and entire enterprises together.

In business, we see the same thing happening: people blindly following P&Ps that may have been relevant at one time but are now clearly outdated. It may take the form of new product introduction steps ("You must follow all nineteen steps"), procedures for the procurement of products or services—even elaborate, trade-marked models for the corporate decision-making process, that all decisions at all levels are supposed to follow.

Manuals become the fiefdom of certain, otherwise powerless, centralized functions, like personnel. These departments occasionally make a religion out of the big book, because it is all they have. Sections are individually dated, amendments are marked, reprints are shipped out once a month—at times one wonders if the true purpose of the organization isn't to maintain up-to-date policy manuals.

Mike once served as a corporate director of communications. The first day on the job, he was escorted to his new digs. He was shown his desk, his phone, his in-box—and then, with a flourish, he was shown the office credenza. It was a black cabinet about five feet wide. Its three shelves were piled deep with successive versions of the company's employee manuals—at least sixty three-ring notebooks, each page of each book noting its date of publication and the page number it was superseding. "These notebooks are our past, our present, and our future," his superior said. "Respect them."

Mike stared at the credenza, open-mouthed. What had he gotten himself into? In retrospect, it would have done that organization a world of good to heap all those manuals into a pile and light up the western sky with them. Manuals are "paper supervisors," a holdover from the pre-team era. Do we still need them at all?

Some kind of on-paper guide to corporate life is necessary. We believe a proper manual should include the basic things team members and other workers need to know about working at a company: its mission, what is expected of employees, and what is promised in return by the organization as a whole. If there is a chain of command, workers need to know what it is. If there are procedures for filing grievances, that is necessary information.

But for heaven's sake, try and keep the manual short. "Manual," after all, implies it should be liftable with a single hand; many of these three-ring P&P frankensteins require a fork-lift to raise off the ground.

Make sure that any P&Ps teams are asked to abide by are relevant and timely. We suggest that teams put expiration dates on policies, just like medicine. On the expiration date, policies are re-examined for relevance. If not relevant, they are flushed, like old penicillin. If they still make sense, the policy prescription is refilled.

Good teams constantly evaluate all their processes, and that includes the rules they follow to get things done. They get rid of (or don't follow) irrelevant ones, modify others as necessary, even create new ones of their own to achieve more effective, more efficient outcomes.

In addition, during the sanity checking of P&Ps, good teams take a stab at identifying barriers (people, processes, structures) which may be getting in the way of achieving desired outcomes. They continuously identify and strategize ways around these barriers as a regular way of doing team business.

Sometimes, a bonfire is in order. This is essentially what happened at the two big car success stories of the past decade, Ford Taurus and GM Saturn. Ford and GM each looked at its baseline, decided it was too screwed up to build upon, and so built entirely new divisions, and made a fresh, honest start in the policies and procedures area. The fresh start gave both of these "skunkworks" projects terrific vitality and a head-start toward success.

*Policies and procedures are supposed
to serve the team, not the other way around.*

chapter 9

•

the people problem

•

i'm not working for that jerk!

When we think about teams, we picture the perfect team. Members are autonomous, intelligent, generous-minded, quick to fill in where another leaves off. They fall somewhere between angels and the drawn characters in apparel ads.

Ideal teams are comprised of perfect people, whose egos and individuality have been subsumed into the greater goal of the team. Real teams—your teams—are made up of living, breathing, and very imperfect people. Chances are good your team includes some real weirdos. Our experience is that, in the forming stage especially, nearly all team members are taken aback by the personalities of other team members. X is a nerd, Y is certifiable, and Z is a blowhard jerk.

That's what we have to work with on teams, and that is a big, big reason teams fail. To keep teams from self-destructing on the basis of personality differences, conflicts, and misunderstandings, we have to move beyond first impressions, beyond expectations of apparel-ad perfection, into the muck and mire of what it is to be a human being, and how to tolerate those who are not as marvelous as ourselves.

The logic of misunderstanding

Even the best teams suffer continuous setbacks because of simple misunderstandings. What we intend to communicate (what we transmit) is seldom exactly what we succeed in communicating (what the other party receives).

Why does this happen? In a word, diversity. We all have different minds, different slants, different hot buttons. We come from different cultures, both ethnic and familial. We share different histories. We have different brains inside our heads.

When the message transmitted is not the message received, the result is not usually an obvious catastrophe. It is more like a plane that is subtly out of control. It won't crash, and it will stay in the air. People on the plane will think they are succeeding, because miles are rolling by on the odometer. Passengers stare out the windows, maybe even waving, confident they are en route to their destination, even as they fly further and further off-course.

> *I know you think you understand*
> *what you thought I said.*
> *But I am not sure that what you heard*
> *is what I meant.*

Every year we flush billions of dollars through our organizations, sunk costs caused by the kinds of everyday misunderstandings and ambiguities we all participate in every day. The worst part of this incredible waste is that we learn next to nothing from it. In our minds it is always the other person's fault for mistransmitting or misreceiving. We are the good one; they are the jerk. Whereas, in reality, there is no good or bad one in a classic miscommunication. It is the child of both parents.

Misunderstandings often occur for the simple reason that the individuals involved are communicating on two different wavelengths. How you communicate with others is influenced to a very large degree by what kind of person you are—by your behavioral style.

Preventing miscommunication means being very alert to your own behavioral style as well as to the style of the person you are talking to.

It requires that we relearn how to communicate with others in a way that is cognizant of their differing natures and sensitive of their needs.

Happy talk and human variation

The picture-perfect team of magazine articles doesn't exist. Indeed, the cheerful attitude that typifies books, articles, and presentations about teams is misleading. Teams cannot solve all your organization's problems. Nothing can.

The horrible truth is that the people on your teams will be like people everywhere. They may be smart in one or two areas but normal or below normal in other ways—ways that have a bearing on your team success. Team members have their ups and downs. You will have team members that are clinically depressed or have serious personality disorders. You will have team members that you can't stand.

You will have team members that might once have been terrific contributors but whose brains simply have lost efficiency. Their neurotransmitters don't fire with the rapidity or regularity that they did fifteen years earlier, or before they were damaged by alcohol, or an accident.

You will go home thinking you have the greatest team in the world, and find out the next morning that one of your stars has been arrested, or is dead. You will have team members whose judgment varies widely from day to day—a sage on Monday, a fool on Tuesday.

These are depressing realities. We say them not to discourage you but to remind you that your on-the-job team problems are just a slice of the problems of life itself. The happy talk articles won't tell you that. We just did.

People are not the same. They are as different as thumbprints. And not just in one way, preferring white or dark turkey meat, or being vegetarian. People are different up and down, through and through, coming and going—in their likes, dislikes, fears, joys, the way they think and decide, the way they work and communicate. Teams succeed when they acknowledge this fact of natural variation and work to recognize and value differences among team members.

It often happens, when we start talking about different personality types, that some cheerful person will suggest the Myers-Briggs Type

Inventory (MBTI) as a tool. The MBTI tells you how you see yourself and gives you a set of label initials to wear through life (ISTJ, ENSP, etc.). It has become a kind of psychological parlor game. Lots of people have taken the test, and the initials they receive help them understand themselves—and forgive people born with different characteristics. It is a very interesting system, especially valuable for the task of self-discovery.

But how you see yourself or how you really are inside doesn't matter much to teams. How you behave on the outside, how you treat other people and how you demand to be treated, does matter. After all, we're not trying to fix our souls, just reduce miscommunications, straighten out a few confusing behaviors, and get people working together more effectively.

In the work world, we could generally give two hoots what a person's insides are like. That is their business, after all. But how they act—and interact—is essential to their value to the enterprise. You don't have to like one another to produce together. You do have to "get along."

David Merril, a Denver psychologist, describes people as falling into four approximate behavioral profiles or zones.[1] It is a very handy way to think about behavioral differences. One of these four behavior zones is, for you, a kind of "home plate"—a place where, day in and day out, other people see you as occupying. The four home plates together make up a big square, like the one on page 55.

Think of the diagram as a map of the personality universe, with a distinct north, south, east, and west. From left to right it measures assertiveness, from reactive passivity to proactive activity, or from "asking" to "telling." From top to bottom it measures responsiveness, whether we react in a controlled task-oriented fashion (top) or in an emotional people-oriented fashion (bottom). Thus a "driver" is a combination of task-oriented and proactive. An "expressive" is a combination of proactive and people-oriented. An "amiable" is people-oriented and reactive, and an "analytical" is a combination of reactive and task-oriented.

---

[1] From conversations with David Merril of Tracom, Denver.

Analytical	Driver
Key Value: Work with existing circumstances to promote quality in products and services	**Key Value:** Shape the environment by overcoming opposition to get immediate results
Orientation: Thinking	**Orientation:** Action
Time: Past	**Time:** Present
Amiable	Expressive
Key Value: Cooperate with others, make sure people are included and feel good about the process	**Key Value:** Shape the environment by bringing others into alliance to generate enthusiasm for the results
Orientation: Relationships	**Orientation:** Intuition
Time: Depends on who they are with at the time	**Time:** Future

As we paint a mental picture of each of the four types, be thinking about which type people see you as.

☛ **Analyticals** are essentially perfectionists, people who serve no wine, take no precipitous action, before its time. The very best thing about analyticals is that, nine times out of ten, they are right about things, because they gave the matter their time, reflection, and rational consideration. Their strong suit is the facts. Their key virtue is patience, and it may also be their downfall—a kind of caution that paralyzes, not from fear but from a determination to fully understand a problem before moving toward a solution. Pushed to the brink, the response of the Analytical is usually to run for cover, until the shooting stops. Adjectives that are sometimes attached to Analyticals: *critical, indecisive, stuffy, picky, moralistic, industrious, persistent, serious, expecting, orderly.*

☛ **Amiables** are essentially "people people," considerate of other people, and very empathic. They are the "warm fuzzies" of the world. Their orientation is the past, the present, and the future—wherever people have needs, and may be hurt. They are the world's best coordinators precisely because they take time to touch base with all parties. Sure, they have opinions—but they may be more interested to know yours. Their great strength is their understanding of relationships. Pushed to the brink, their response is usually to cave in. Adjectives that are sometimes attached to Amiables: *conforming, unsure, ingratiating, dependent, awkward, supportive, respectful, willing, dependable, agreeable.*

☛ **Drivers** are essentially let-me-do-it people. They are firmly rooted in the present moment, and they are lovers of action. Their great strength: results. If you want a job discussed, talk to one of the other three types; if you just want it done, take it to a Driver. They aren't much for inner exploration, but they sure bring home the bacon. They can be bitterly self-critical, and resentful of idle chit-chat. Favorite song: "Steamroller Blues." Pushed to the brink, Drivers become tyrants. Adjectives that are sometimes attached to Drivers: *pushy, severe, tough, dominating, harsh, strong-willed, independent, practical, decisive, efficient.*

☛ **Expressives** are essentially big-picture people, always looking for a fresh perspective on the world around them. They are future-oriented, perhaps because that is where no one can ever pin them down as they dream their grand dreams. If you want a straight answer, Expressives may not be the best place to turn. If you want intuition and creativity, they're perfect. If you want a terrific party, invite lots of Expressives. Pushed to the brink, Expressives can react savagely, by attacking. Though cheerful nine ways out of ten, they take the world they create in their heads very seriously. Adjectives that are sometimes attached to Expressives: *manipulating, excitable, undisciplined, reacting, egotistical, ambitious, stimulating, wacky, enthusiastic, dramatic, friendly.*

Now, on teams, we are likely to find all these behavioral types mixed together and expected to communicate. This is not an irrational expectation—we are all carbon-based lifeforms, we are all featherless bipeds, and we mostly speak the same language.

But come on—putting an Analytical in the same room with an Expressive? A Driver with an Amiable? A Driver with an Expressive? Imagine a triple date featuring, oh . . .

- Isaac Newton and Madonna
- George Patton and Oprah Winfrey
- Cleopatra and Pee Wee Herman

. . . and you get an idea that there might be a few breaks in the conversation. They might all adore each other, but generally speaking, these types are so different in outlook (and in inlook) that in combination with one another they are often incompatible, and even toxic. Chances are that you are on a team right now that includes, in subtle shadings, a Patton, a Newton, a Winfrey. Chances are excellent that teams this diverse are experiencing real communication problems.

We can't solve all the communication snafus your entire team is experiencing, but we can help you straighten out your own communications with the others. First, identify your communication style. Do you come across to others as an Analytical, Amiable, Driver, or Expressive? Probably you accept one of the four designations, but reluctantly, because of the negatives associated with each.

Second, adapt your style to suit the needs of whoever you're communicating with. Can you change your style? Yes and no. To go from being one style to its opposite—from a pure Analytical to a pure Expressive—would probably make your head explode. But you can soften the extremeness of your style, and learn how to communicate with people in other styles.

Here are some tips to help you make the empathic crossing to each of the four styles.

With *Drivers*, strive to:

- Be brief and to the point. Think "efficiency."
- Stick to business. Skip the chit-chat. Close loopholes. Dispel ambiguities. Digress at your peril. Speculate and you're history.
- Be prepared. Know the requirements and objectives of the task at hand.
- Organize your arguments into a neat "package." Present your facts cleanly and logically.

- Be courteous, not chummy. Don't be bossy—Drivers may not themselves be driven.
- Ask specific questions. Do not go "fishing" for answers.
- If you disagree, disagree with the facts, not the person.
- If you agree, support the results *and* the person.
- Persuade by citing objectives and results. Outcomes rule!
- When finished, leave. No loitering.

With *Expressives*, strive to:

- Meet their social needs while talking shop. Entertain, stimulate, be lively.
- Talk about their goals as well as the team's.
- Be open—strong and silent does not cut it with expressives.
- Take time. They are most efficient when not in a hurry.
- Ask for their opinions and ideas.
- Keep your eye on the big picture, not the technical details.
- Support your points with examples involving people they know and respect.
- Offer special deals, extras, and incentives.
- Show honest respect—you must not talk down to an Expressive.

With *Amiables*, strive to:

- Break the ice—it shows your commitment to the task and to them.
- Show respect. Amiables will be hurt by any attempt to patronize.
- Listen and be responsive. Take your time. Learn the whole story.
- Be nonthreatening, casual, informal. A crisp, commanding style will send Amiables packing.
- Ask "how" questions to draw out their opinions.
- Define what you want them to contribute to the task.
- Assure and guarantee that the decision at hand will in no way risk, harm or threaten others. But make no assurances you can't back up.

With *Analyticals*, strive to:

- Prepare your case in advance.
- Take your time, but be persistent.

- Support their principles. Show you value their thoughtful approach.
- Cover all bases. Do not leave things to chance, or hope "something good happens."
- Draw up a scheduled approach for any action plan. Be specific on roles and responsibilities.
- Be clear. Disorganization or sloppiness in presentation is a definite turn-off.
- Avoid emotional arguments. No wheedling or cajoling. No pep rallies.
- Follow through. The worst thing you can do with an Analytical is break your word, because they will remember.

○○○

What we are urging is not that you be a chameleon, changing your color to match the color of whoever you are dealing with. Rather, that you try to see things through their eyes, and understand their needs and preferences.

It is critical for people with weaknesses in one area—e.g., visionary people tend to go limp in the nuts-and-bolts department—to either delegate authority or to redouble their efforts to think practically. It is equally critical, in ordinary communication, for one type to know what another type is listening for.

You are not a rat in a box that can make only one response to every stimulus. You are a human being, with a host of choices in every situation. We are urging that you choose to be curious about other people's natures and needs and accommodate them when possible. When you do this, you will find them accommodating you in return. This reciprocal accommodation is just another dimension of teamwork.

Dealing with difficult people

So far in this chapter we have talked about the normal range of personality issues that can impinge on team performance. So long as intentions are good, people in this normal range have an excellent chance of communicating accurately. Unfortunately, there exist several types of people whose intentions may not be as good, and whose behavior is just not malleable. They call for special treatment.

Team jerks

On any given day, we can all be jerks—rude people who are unaware how they come across. But the true team jerk goes beyond occasional jerkiness to full-blown jerkhood. They are jerks par excellence. Compared to them, we are amateurs.

A team jerk is usually its most talented member. He or she may have made some very important contributions to the enterprise. Their specialty is ideas—new technologies, new products, new processes, new applications, new combinations of existing things, marketing ideas. Extraordinarily bright and creative, they are high-achieving dynamos when motivated, giving off ideas the way regular folk emit carbon dioxide.

Take Bert (please!). He is a prima donna about his talent. He won't play by the rules other team members follow. He demands that other people attend to him, while he ignores them. Communication with him has eroded to the point where the team simply ignores him—yet hopes he includes them the next time a great idea comes to him. When team members do try to include him in things, he brushes them off.

A good archetype for Bert is the software programmer who is a genius with C++, but has horrendous social skills. You hate to lose his talent, but you could sure do without his arrogance, his eccentricities, and his contempt. Wouldn't hurt if he bathed a bit more often, either.

What can you do with a guy like Bert? First, acknowledge that his personality is not his fault. None of us asks to be born with the precise set of talents and peculiarities we get. The jerk is often blessed with great creativity but cursed with a crummy personality.

There are two strong opposing forces in the creative person. The one force is that person's internal standards, which are precious and, in many ways, the secret to that person's success. At all costs, the creative jerk tells himself, he must be true to that inner measure. The other force is one we are more familiar with—the drive we all have for recognition by others. The problem is that the two forces don't reconcile all that easily. Especially bright people have to struggle to know which drive to honor at any given moment.

Second, appreciate that what you see is probably not all there is. People who act arrogant often have profound insecurities. People who laugh in your face may well cry when you are gone. These people may simply be failing to adequately communicate what is going on inside them. The sad secret of many creative types is that they are experiencing more stress and more pain than other team members.

In addition, an individual who is susceptible to the terrible pressures of the workplace is probably not immune to pressures on the home front, either. It's possible that behind the superficial inappropriate behavior may lurk problems far more difficult to solve—marital conflicts, chemical abuse, mental illness. Historically, creative geniuses have always had a knack for turning their right-brain talents against themselves.

Third, see if the team itself is helping to create the problem. Maybe team members unconsciously "out" a jerk because he is cut from such a different bolt of cloth than they are. Or maybe the team rules and policies are too narrow to accommodate a personality with extra, um, verve.

Having made these adaptations, however, you still have the problem of Bert being Bert. You can change the whole world to suit some people, and they will continue to be jerks.

Here's a radical idea: Why not ask him what he would like? Ask if he wants to continue as a team member. Ask him if there is anything he would like done differently—whom to report to, when and how often to meet, whether to work side by side or from remote locations.

Make clear that you are searching for a solution that enables him to keep being himself, and doing the quality of work he does, and making some kind of contribution to the team—and that alleviates the personality clashes that are making everyone miserable. If he perceives himself to be at war with the team, he may be very wary of such a pow-wow. So you must be very supporting, yet very candid with him.

The solution may be to redesignate him. Set him apart from the core team, as a valued resource team member. Make him a unit unto himself, with a dotted-line relationship to the team, as a reference source, sounding board, or technology guru. Set him up as a one-man skunkworks. Give him an office in a separate building, or on a separate continent, even. Buy him some bunny slippers and make a telecommuter out of him.

Be careful about sending your genius off to the jungle by himself, however. The idea of separation may sound good to both him and to the team, but it may backfire. It's very likely that Bert needs human contact to keep from going completely insane or becoming depressed. The team he derides and ignores may be his lifeline.

Perhaps the best solution is for the team to accept the fact that it needs Bert and Bert, though he gives little indication of this, needs the team. Why not make a concerted effort to give Bert what he needs—admiration, support, and sympathy? Just because he doesn't act especially human doesn't mean he is immune to human feelings. We all need a kind word from time to time and the occasional reassuring pat on the back.

Now that you have his attention, let your newfound appreciation be the basis on which a new alliance can be built between the individual and you. Once he sees you are a true fan, you can do something. Acknowledge his talents, put an arm around his shoulder and say, "Hey, if we're going to let that talent blossom, we have to do something about these self-defeating behaviors."

Don't apply the medicine, the behavioral change, until you have first proffered the candy of encouragement and fellow-feeling. And when the time comes to name those self-defeating obnoxious behaviors, be specific. It's no good using value-laden, broadbrush terms like *jerk, arrogant, obtuse sonofabitch*, etc.

Instead, say:

- "It appears to me that you shoot from the hip during the meetings, and you hurt people's feelings and make enemies."
- "It appears to me that you can't take criticism. When I asked you about your design at Thursday's meeting, you got up and left the room."
- "It seems as if you like making cruel jokes, and you don't know how bad that makes people feel."
- "Julie, the transcriptionist, quit because you yelled at her."

- "I left six messages on your voicemail and you never got back to me."
- "You play Guns 'n Roses when the rest of us are trying to read professional journals."

The creative high-achiever has a hot pilot light. He or she burns hotter and works harder than most people. And where all of us have an inner core that we descend into from time to time in our lives, the creative high-achiever virtually camps out there, intensely focused on whatever it is that he or she is striving to create or achieve. They are almost of another race than the rest of us—us being turtles and them being racehorses. Small wonder if adapting to our hobbling pace causes them problems.

One thing about them is that you can't help them by slowing them down. Stress for them may actually be lower when their activity level is hyper or beyond. Never tell a racehorse to walk a few laps. Creatives and high achievers are often subspecies of workaholics, and workaholics have a way of dying within a year of retirement.

Can people, whether they are genius-jerks or whatever, really get hold of their basic natures and change them? How many teams have ever witnessed the kind of transformation necessary to turn around a career?

And even when the results are good, the process may not be over. A team member who has alienated everyone on the team will find that his transformation is not universally trusted. Like the boy who cried wolf too often, the genius-no-longer-(such)-a-jerk will find that many colleagues are hard to win over. There is a degree to which people almost prefer the two-dimensionality of poor behavior to the unpredictability of more sensitive behavior. So more has to change sometimes than just the individual. Sometimes the team has to change with him (or her).

Team blowhards

In the old Aesop fairy tale, one thing stood between a houseful of mice and complete happiness—the cat. So the mice met and voted to eliminate the danger forever, by tying a bell around the cat's neck. With the bell in place, the cat would be unable to sneak up on and devour another mouse. The only problem was getting volunteers to tie the bell on.

The same goes with teams. Nearly every team has one member, either a leader or a peer, who cannot seem to help dominating team activities. Even when time is short and the agenda is crowded, these blowhards feel they have to get their share of attention. Team blowhards talk too often, too long, are impossible to shut up, enjoy initiating distractions, and just generally dominate team proceedings.

What can the team do to suppress these people? Putting a bell on them doesn't work—we saw it tried once, and, well, the blowhards just take it off. But there are other solutions.

The most conventional solutions are managerial in nature. They are old-fashioned, autocratic, pre-team remedies by which the team leader shuts up the noisy and encourages the quiet. The most drastic is to simply terminate the overbearing offender. Termination may seem like the perfect weapon in all kinds of team personality issues, but beware. Termination:

- is unfair; you're effectively dismissing someone for overcontributing.
- is potentially litigious; nothing like a team lawsuit to bring folks together.
- subtly undermines the authority of the team leader; it shows you can't manage a simple situation.
- is inefficient; you have thrown out the baby with the bathwater, wasted a whole team member to eliminate a single flaw.

Some teams "quarantine" overbearing members; they redesignate them as wing units to get them out of the home office. But here again, keeping expressive people at home—banning them from the regular environment—wastes talent. Meanwhile, it's nearly always a bad idea to change a job description to suit an individual.

In meetings, some team leaders "bell the bully" by artificially ostracizing them from the team process, by assigning them the task of flipping the flipcharts, or manning the lightswitch at the back of the room. If a bully is talking, it is possible to talk through them—the inappropriate sound of two voices vying for attention gets even the biggest bully's attention.

Some team leaders turn their backs to the overtalker—you don't reinforce what you don't see. You can simply ignore them. If they are constantly raising hands, don't look their way. If they interrupt, smile and say—"Let's look at that later."

Call on other team members to help. "Come on, gang, let's not let Audrey here do all the work. Who else has an idea? Who agrees with Audrey? Disagrees?"

If the bully seems unmoved by all these attempts, take them aside during a break and tell them in no uncertain terms: "You are dragging the group away from the agenda. If you keep this up, the team will be a joke. If you can't adjust to the agenda, you're not welcome here."

The most important tool in combating distraction is the team agenda. Make your agenda central, and stick to it at all costs. If someone goes off on a tangent, pull them back. An agenda keeps you from being the "bad person." You say, "George, that is really very interesting, but it is not what we agreed to discuss today." Let the agenda take the heat for disciplining the process. You're not disagreeing—you're just keeping things on track.

If someone is dominating, they still have to breathe. When they stop for that breath, leap in, and say, "George, that's interesting—can we relate that to the agenda before us?" You can also simply say, "George, that's interesting, but let me hear from other people, too." And then you turn your eye contact away and poll others for opinions.

Some team leaders take preemptive action—heading the bully off at the pass, before he or she ruins the team. The more you can do before a team get-together, hammering out an understanding of the tasks at hand, the better the meeting will go. He who controls the minutes controls the meeting.

There are social solutions to the problem of blowhards—ways of communicating that overtalkers need to turn it down, and undertalkers need to summon the courage to speak. Consider throwing the bully a bone. People who want attention can sometimes be satisfied—or frightened away—with a little. Say, "Good idea, Jack. Anybody else?" It doesn't have to be a big bone. But never appease a bully with flattery ("Roy, you have so many wonderful ideas!"). Positive reinforcement only invites more of the reinforced behavior.

The worst person to have in a team is the negative thinker. "We tried that, and it didn't work," is this person's bludgeon. One tactic is to turn that person's negativity around: "How would you make it work this time?" "How can we overcome those obstacles?"

The imbalance between shy people and demonstrative people can be a major problem for team interaction. How do you achieve the team ideal—everyone participating, everyone contributing—if one person drowns out three others? A skilled team manager knows how to keep from being steamrollered by compulsive hard-driving Type A behavior; by authoritarian personalities who think it is just fitting and natural that others should obey them; and by "Machiavellian manipulators," people who are on the lookout for a neck to sharpen their axe on—yours.

Throw in the cultural and attitudinal deference often given to males, to people with booming voices, to tall people, and the natural advantage of seniority on the company flow-chart, and there is a lot to overcome.

Team leaders need to plan solutions to these problems in advance. Structure the information so that people know, when the team meeting starts, what is expected of them, what is permitted, and what is out of line. Announce that you want everyone's input, not just one or two people's. With that understanding in mind, individuals are less likely to hijack the team.

Challenge them to prove that their point of view is substantive, that they have something relevant to say, and are not just talking to hear their tongues flap. Look them dead in the eye and ask them, "If you could make your point in 25 words, what would it be?"

Try to win them to your side. "I like what you are saying, but I have only a short time to make my points here—could I go first?" If necessary, shut the blowhard down. "I have no idea what the answer to the question of parking privileges is—I'm here to talk about the team's strategy."

One strategy is to "equalize" group membership through something called the nominal group technique. Here the facilitator asks group members to quietly write down what their thoughts are on the coming meeting. Then the facilitator reads the ideas, and thus controls group input. This approach can be linked with electronic meeting tools, which we will discuss in a later chapter.

Team brats

Judith Bardwick, in her book *Danger in the Comfort Zone* (AMACOM, 1991), describes an attitude that has crept gradually into the workplace in recent years—and one that spells unavoidable death to successful teaming. She calls the attitude entitlement. It is a team member's feeling that the rest of the team, or the organization as a whole, owes him or her membership. If entitlement is too abstract a phrase, consider the one your parents used when you acted like that at age 5—spoiled brat.

In the old days there was no spoiled brat syndrome because no organization spoiled its workers, except for the few lucky ones at the top. But in our century there has slowly evolved a belief—and it is shared by many nations, and many systems, from capitalism to communism—that people have an inherent right to fair treatment, a living wage, and decent conditions.

That doesn't sound too bad. In fact, you probably want to agree that those things should be guaranteed to all people. The problem is that as these assumptions have evolved, they have become sloppy, and people—human nature being what it is—have taken advantage. Lots of people in lots of organizations decided that the new contract between organizations and team members should put the entire onus for doing on the organization, and none on the team member.

People too often are too comfortable and have too little responsibility. For years, people have been succeeding individually without necessarily contributing to the success of their teams.

Brattism says: "I have what I have because the team owes it to me. I get it simply by existing, not by doing." Spoiled Brat Syndrome happens at every level. It is the CEO holding out for a $5 million bonus and a golden parachute compensation plan, despite unprofitability for investors and ruthless downsizing for workers. It is the shortsighted investor, only interested in what an investment nets for him, not in what the business makes or does. It is the perks and plush carpets of Congressional offices during budgetary cutbacks. It is unions demanding 95 percent of salary for workers when they are not working.

At the team level, brattism is team members waiting for someone else to show leadership, to volunteer, to share information, to take chances. It is people hiding behind functions ("I'm in marketing, you need to talk to sales"). It is complaining about compensation when the team has not produced anything worthwhile for the organization. It is teams with poorly formed objectives and goals performing pointless tasks they know have no value or utility, all the while insisting they are burning the midnight oil.

The terrible irony is that the utopian idea of providing a more secure life for workers has too often undermined the American dream. Brattism is a primary cause of bloat, bureaucracy, turf wars, indifferent service and shoddy product quality.

It is also the cause of a shift in our character, of our ethics, a point Bardwick made in her book. When we are not held to account for our actions, it is easy to rationalize our shortcomings:

> *No one else is working hard, so why should I?*
> *If no one catches you, you didn't anything wrong.*
> *A job not worth doing is not worth doing well.*

How does a team combat incipient brattism? Through vigilance and intolerance. By keeping the team on track to achieve their stated objectives, and by making sure those objectives are actually achievable.

Team members slip into brattism for two main reasons—the team's objectives are unachievable, or they are too easily achieved. Teams require just the right degree of engagement, or members rebel and drift into defiant anti-team attitudes.

Restoring a team from brattism to honest engagement doesn't happen without leadership. The first order for leaders is to clear away any vestige of brattism at the top. No team is going to come clean and shed its bad attitudes while the team at the top is permitted to continue with its own.

The leader then administers pressure. People perform or they depart. But the pressure must be to achieve a very specific outcome. Rewards must be for achievements that matter, not digging and refilling holes. People must feel their work is important. People who cannot make the crossing to be more accountable even with training must be winnowed out and replaced.

The passage from an attitude of brattism to earning is not an easy one. It requires pain and anxiety, by definition. Brattism is like dope that numbs us to the twinges of reality. But at the end of this anxious exodus is the possibility of great success and great fulfillment. The feeling of achieving this possible success makes the aches and pains worthwhile.

Dark angels

There are people out there who should not be on any team, anywhere, ever. We are not referring to reclusives or the terminally shy. They can participate. We are talking about the organizational equivalent of the undead. If you follow the medical model, you would say they are sociopathic. If you are a strict moralist you will call them evil. If you lean more toward the supernatural, you might call them dark angels.

A dark angel can take several forms:

✔ *The addict.* Who acts crazy because of some personal problem

✔ *The ogre.* Who acts out of antisocial rage

✔ *The crook.* Who thinks nothing of crossing ethical lines

✔ *The fanatic* Who puts achieving his objectives above all rules and policies

Here's what a dark angel can do.

A team of five was set up to study the feasibility of direct marketing a new product. Everyone on the team seemed to have a reasonable amount of team spirit, except for Roger. Which was strange because Roger, a mail order whiz, begged to be part of the team.

Soon, the sabotage began. Reports that had been carefully proofread went out with embarrassing errors. Schedules that had been carefully synchronized were now way off—people began showing up for meetings on the wrong day, or for meetings that the other party was unaware of. The networking software went down. Even the petty cash account was off, by almost $50.

Everyone was confused. At first it seemed like phenomenally bad luck. But after a crucial file disappeared from the server hard disk, they began pointing fingers. When accused, Roger gave them his best, "What? Me?" face, denied everything, and declared he was deeply offended at any suggestion he would undermine the team. And hadn't his schedule been shuffled as well? He was the victim, not the perpetrator.

He was persuasive. It wasn't until a bit of e-mail from one of Roger's previous team members surfaced, asking if the team were experiencing any data problems, that Roger was confronted again. No one could understand his motive. It wasn't for promotion, or to make himself look good, or personal vendetta. He was just a crazy, rotten guy. An ogre, who hated his life, his team, his job—everything. An unapologetic wrecker of well-laid plans.

People in human resources consulting will tell you how to handle all kinds of personnel issues. But no one's got much of a handle on what to do with a dark angel like Roger. Dark angels are the beasties in the New Age box, the team poison pill. The brave new world we've been ushering in didn't plan on their being there. But there they are.

There often isn't a lot of incentive to get rid of dark angels. Terminating people is confrontative, unpleasant, and potentially litigious. So we look the other way and hope the madness goes away. A team member with an addict personality may collapse from the weight of his or her own problems. A team member with an ogre personality, driven by some dark rage, may still be a good producer. Team members who go berserk and start hurling large objects about the office telekinetically—well, who are they bothering really?

A team member who is unscrupulous or super-competitive or overzealous is doing exactly what he thinks he was hired to do. Be honest — amoral unscrupulousness is a tried, true pathway to success in many organizations.

Explaining the ten commandments to them won't stop these people. Philosopher and social critic Scott Peck[2] theorizes that evil is not a choice we make but an external force with its own reality, seeking opportunities, viruslike, where it can find them. And it finds them most often in isolated, alienated individuals, who are so

---

[2] Scott Peck, *People of the Lie* (New York: Simon & Schuster), 1983.

estranged by upbringing, circumstance, or by their very nature that no act is beneath them as they roll unstoppably toward their objectives.

Some people you can counsel, some you can transfer to the company office in Ultima Thule. Some you can quietly let go, and let their sins paddle off to some new ship to wreck—you may even write the delicately phrased letter of recommendation ("I cannot recommend Kennedy too highly.").

But some people, like the alien being hiding in your hold, leave you one option. A stake through the heart, before they put one through you.

The will to team

Most personalities, we conclude, fall within the normal range, and can be dealt with if we simply acknowledge our differences and learn what we all want from one another. Once we get that out of the way, we can go to work and earn some money.

When you start to know people, it's easier to root for them. We want the team to succeed not just for the team's sake, but for everyone's sake. That's the foundation of team spirit right there—learning combined with the *willingness* to act upon what we learn.

This will to team doesn't sound like much, but it's critical to team success. Without it, all the training, rewards and recognitions, meetings, pronouncements, consultants, weekend retreats, etc., are worthless. No team can be a team against its will.

Teams achieve this "willing" state only one way—by learning about one another and by caring. Both must occur. Where there is no learning, no knowledge, no information, there can be no caring. But if people have made up their minds not to give a damn, neither can there be any learning.

So shape up out there, all you teams. You don't have to like one another especially. But in a way you do have to get to know one another, and to value one another's abilities and individuality. Meet them halfway with your respect and understanding, and together you can move the team objectives forward.

part three

•

what

keeps

teams

from

working

chapter 10

•

leadership failure

•

who's in charge here, anyway?

Leadership is the most used word in organizational literature. It bears the burden for so much of every organization's hopes. Everyone agrees that leadership is vital to teams, the chlorophyll that permits the making of sugar. But what is it, exactly, and how does a team without it get it?

When a team is in trouble, its leadership is very often the problem. One of the best ways to understand leadership is by seeing what happens when it isn't there. It isn't pretty.

Things aren't happening. Managers resort to a machine approach to getting work out the door. "When in doubt, automate." People are upset, disillusioned, hostile to their own enterprise. If work does get done it has a predictable character—it is half-assed. There is genuine despair among the team because there is no rallying point, no one to vent at, no one to intercede when things go awry and get everyone back on track.

Team members get angry at one another; eventually they either explode in anger or implode in despair. Or worst of all, they decay in a lifeless orbit. Commitment and energy drain away. Slowly, individuals begin to drift away from the team. By the time the team figures out it's dead, it's really dead.

If that sounds like everything bad that can happen to a team, you're right. Leadership is *that* important. This chapter is going to take an extra-long look at what makes a good team leader, how the team can help its leader lead, and suggest some new ways of leading that you may not have thought of. Indeed, if leadership is vigorous and intact, few other problems are insurmountable. But from a practical standpoint, few organizations have figured out:

- what team leadership is exactly
- how to foster it
- where it ends and autonomous teamwork begins

Let's look at two actual individuals we know, and the kind of leadership they embody.

Ted H.: Hard Charger

Ted is a "Chief," a front-line supervisor of baggage handlers, for a major U.S. airline. His assigned turf is the plane servicing ramps at Denver's international airport. At least, it's supposed to be. Just as often, one finds Ted at the airline's executive offices, or elsewhere in the system, helping to remedy everything from employee motivation and training issues to knotty baggage and service problems.

Everyone is struck by Ted's energy and his ideas for improvement. His station manager describes him as a prototypical "sparkplug." He is technically competent and highly effective as a supervisor. But, his manager notes, Ted's real value is that he is always looking for ways to improve baggage handling performance—even flying to other stations from time to time, to work on inter-unit problems.

He's one of those infectious people. He gets you involved, one way or another, either directly by collaring you and hitting you up for ideas or resources, or indirectly, as a model. As one of his peers comments, Ted's motto just seems to be: "Lead, follow, join, or step aside . . . there are things to be done." Ted would probably put it more graphically.

Ted once appeared at his boss's office door, excused himself for barging in, then proceeded to outline what he felt were significant reasons for poor baggage handling and supervisory performance. Ted indicated he was willing to help get together a system-wide group of chiefs like himself and noodle the problems and possible grassroots solutions. So—did the boss suppose such an effort would enjoy executive support?

Somehow, the boss knew, senior management did not have whatever it took to discourage Ted.

Jim S.: Quiet Warrior

Jim's an engineering manager for a major lawn equipment manufacturer. He's a quiet, unassuming kind of guy, sporting your basic trademark rolled sleeve white shirts and "pocket protector." You might not immediately place him as the motivating power behind a lot of cross-functional teamwork and innovative approaches to product development. But that's what he is.

Harvey got to know Jim when he participated in a company-sponsored leadership workshop. Jim was one of a very few holding up a hand to the question: "Did anyone here volunteer for this program?"

As Harvey sought to better understand the company's various internal customer service processes, Jim's name kept cropping up in many quarters as a positive example. Intrigued, Harvey did a little digging for specifics. As it turned out, Jim had been quietly but effectively leveraging both the human and physical assets of the company for some time. He had taken over a group whose efforts were behind schedule, over cost, and ridden with quality problems—and transformed the last nine projects into winners by any standard.

These were not laboratory successes. In each case, Jim had to work with different resources organized into many different cross-functional teams. This isn't always a prescription for collaborative effort; yet, many actually reported they were "having fun." When folks were asked how Jim was able to accomplish these startling results, they said things like: "helped us to focus" . . . "a lot of personal energy" . . . "helped us get, analyze, and share information" . . . "supported our creativity" . . . and "helped us to discover and stay on the most productive path."

So what can you say about Ted and Jim? Their stories sound a little—um—incredible. It's true, they are. To us, and to the teams they work with, Ted and Jim are inspirational. They are capable. They are dogged in their pursuit of a better way. And they are so genuine, so enthusiastic, that other people just want to climb aboard.

They are the real thing, and there is much they can teach us, just by being out there on the front lines taking care of business and visible. They startle us by being real, and in doing so they dispel a bushel basket of leadership myths.

Myths of team leadership

It's easy to think of team leadership the wrong way. For instance: "Give our team a good leader and everything will be A-OK." There are a ton of unwarranted assumptions lurking in that statement.

Assumption: *Teams require a single individual to lead them.* It isn't so. There are many models of team leadership, ranging from traditional iron-hand rule through various degrees of self-direction to apparent leaderlessness. Leadership can rotate by the clock, or by the task at hand.

Assumption: *Strong leadership ensures success.* It isn't so. Strong leadership is useless if the people following the leader are incompetent or uninterested in the team task. A fundamentally bad team cannot be "led"—except perhaps to a place of execution.

Assumption: *How a leader is selected is not important.* Wrong. Leaders must be selected in a way that is consonant with the task a team is assigned and the kind of team he or she is assigned to. A free-wheeling, autonomous team will not welcome a leader assigned from outside the group. A new leader may have trouble adjusting to an established team. A team never previously allowed to make decisions for itself may be unable to choose its own leaders.

☛ **Assumption:** *Team success is all that matters.* In a narrow sense, sure, team success matters to the team. But team success, whether driven by a strong leader or not, is meaningless if the task was wrong, duplicative, wasteful, pointless.

☛ **Assumption:** *Team structure is a secondary consideration.* It isn't. Every team structure and configuration we are aware of—functionally aligned, cross-functionally aligned, matrix, network, single-leader, multiple-leader, leader-less—is valid, when applied to the appropriate team task. Perfect leadership and perfect followership combined will still come to nothing unless the team is the right type of team for the task at hand.

☛ **Assumption:** *A good leader and a good team can solve any task.* Sorry—not every task is appropriate for team action. If a task shouldn't be done by a team at all, it hardly matters who or how skilled its leader is.

The leadership spectrum

Too often we define or describe leadership when we see it. Leadership in a teaming atmosphere can look like just about anything. It can look like a good old-fashioned, hierarchical, top-down, leader-led team. The leader is the boss, everyone else does what the boss says.

Or, on the opposite end of the spectrum, it can occur on ultra-flattened, inside-out, molecular, so-called leader-less teams. (We prefer the term shared leadership.) No individual is set above any other, but everyone pitches in to keep the team focused and on track.

No single model of leadership is absolutely wrong, and none is absolutely right. A democratic approach is great for achieving buy-in to team decisions. It creates fewer hurt feelings, less resentment, and better morale. But in crises, or for quick-fixes to stop the bleeding or hose down a fire, an autocratic leadership style can be perfect. In a dog-sled race, the human driving the team must be something of a tyrant. In time of war, the military model suddenly makes terrific sense.

At either end of the spectrum, we see good and poor leaders.

Can you "fix" poor leadership?

It is much easier to fix your own leadership deficiencies than it is to fix someone else's. To fix your own, you must simply acknowledge what you will never be good at, and get someone else to take over those leadership dimensions—to share leadership with you. Or you can work to build up and strengthen the weak areas, while drawing upon the team for understanding and assistance.

To get someone else to change is a tall order. People providing poor leadership generally know—sometimes vaguely—they are part of the problem. But in their minds they are convinced they are doing their best, or just behaving the way their personalities allow them to behave. Sure, they could read some book about ultra leadership. But to change, really change? That is a tall order, requiring:

- courage on the intervener's part
- great honesty on the flawed leader's part
- good intentions on the part of everyone

Leadership problems

The following 24 problems can be taken two ways, as problems with your own leadership, or as problems with someone else's leadership. It's a long list, but a complete list of the ways leaders disappoint would be much longer.

✔ *Stupid leaders.* The perception that a leader is stupid is insulting, but worse, it is statistically a very strong likelihood. No company, not even IBM or McKinsey, is immune from hiring the occasional bonehead—someone without the brain talent to understand the task at hand and to communicate it to others.

If the problem is simply low I.Q., it will manifest itself in a number of ways. A leader will make frequent, repeated mistakes, misremembering important facts, coming to wrong conclusions based on evidence at hand. Teams can come to this kind of leader's rescue by dividing some of the tasks of leadership and reassigning them to team members competent in those areas.

But the problem usually isn't simply low I.Q. People low on brainpower seldom advance to positions of leadership. The problem is more often hard-headedness, mental stubbornness—an obdurate unwillingness to listen to alternatives once one course of action has been decided or one perspective has been adopted. Many leaders are—what is the politically correct way to say this—*flexibility challenged.*

There are individuals who have a vexing combination of attributes—they are untalented in the craft of managing but skilled in the politics of leading. If their intentions are good, a team can get by for awhile on their charisma, enthusiasm, personal charm. But team performance will be poor, and these leaders will eventually have to step aside.

If their intentions are bad, the team has a dark angel in its midst—an individual skilled at covering up his or her own failures, at surviving despite team underperformance. This person is a danger to the team's mission, and must be taken out.

✔ *Leaders who are ignorant.* In real life we forgive stupidity and condemn ignorance. On teams, ignorance is preferable.

There are several reasons. First, some ignorance is a given with teams. The days of the all-knowing leader are over. The concept of teams is predicated upon people complementing one another's limited knowledge to create a stronger whole.

Second, ignorance doesn't have to be forever; stupidity, on the other hand, is terminal. We all have gaps in our knowledge base that we can fill in with learning. But there are degrees and kinds of ignorance. You might say that an ignorant mind is an open mind—ready to be filled, open to new information and perspectives. Good ignorance. Humble ignorance.

Bad ignorance is proud of being ignorant, closed off to new input, stuck in its ways. Perhaps it is ignorance founded on experience: "This always worked for me in the past, so I don't need to learn any new approach now."

What can team members do when a leader lacks knowledge critical to leading? Offer to fill in the gaps or to bring in a new team member or co-leader from outside the team. It is a delicate matter, but it must be broached, because teams succeed on their own competencies.

✔ *Overtrained leaders.* This is the eager beaver syndrome. There is a subgenus of team leaders who attend a few too many seminars, read a few too many magazine articles, and are perpetually bubbling over with the desire to set aside current initiatives and replace them with new, improved ones. To put it simply, the team leader is learning too quickly to integrate what he or she is learning.

Objecting to this eagerness can be perilous—one can easily appear "anti-progress," or "change-resistant." Make it clear that learning is valued—but as a means, not an end.

✔ *Leaders who are too talented.* This is a problem some teams wouldn't mind grappling with—when the leader or leaders are so bright that their personal competence exceeds their ability to teach. It is the "too smart for her own good" syndrome, where the leader is so brilliant the team never catches up. The best example from the literature is probably the Professor on *Gilligan's Island*—smart enough to make a cyclotron out of coconut shells but unable to persuade his crew to patch a boat.

Solution: Change the individual's role from team leader to team resource. Everyone will breathe a sigh of relief.

✔ *Leaders who are too kind.* Sometimes, being considerate is a team leader's downfall. Some leaders begin to see team members as their responsibility, their wards. They worry, "Am I going too fast for them? Am I pushing them too hard?" The danger is that their concern becomes a limiting factor on team progress, with the leader knowing what's best and trying to spare team members the shock of sudden plunges into new territory.

The antidote is for leaders to realize that these are grown men and women, not children or cocker spaniels. Pain and fear are a natural part of learning. Without crossing the line into managerial sadism, a leader is expected to keep team members always on the edge of what is comfortable—always learning.

✔ *Leaders who are closed to new ideas.* This is related to the question about ignorance. Leaders all have, in our managerial make-up, tools with which we have enjoyed consistent success. Like the carpenter poised with hammer, we are ready, willing, and able to find a nail to pound.

The problem is that the workplace is not all nails. The tried and true problem-solving approach isn't applicable to every situation. The best leaders accept this and develop a diverse set of tools, to avoid over-reliance on the hammer. Bad leaders keep hammering away long after the pounding stops doing any good.

This is a learning issue. Leadership must be about learning, openness to knowledge from every quarter. Ostriches are said to stick their heads in the sand when challenged—we think this behavior is much more typical of bad leaders.

How does a team intervene with a closed-minded leader? Good question. A good organization does not seek out such people at any level—but we know that every organization is rife with them. Chances are that the resistance to new ideas is a fear reaction. If the leader has succeeded with Approach A, Approach B will not seem familiar or "succeedable."

This evolution from hammerer to hammerhead is as ancient as the Assyrian bull. Every team must be constantly working to prevent calcification in all its members, but especially its leaders. We suggest creating a culture of conscious and continuous openness—an atmosphere that instinctively rewards looking freshly at new approaches and perspectives, and which is instinctively suspicious of reliance on the tried and the allegedly true.

This is the spirit of continuous improvement—nothing is ever so good that it cannot be made better.

✔ *Leaders with inappropriate styles.* It happens all the time. An empowering type of leader expects team members to function autonomously, with a minimum of direction. But the team either has no experience with this kind of freedom, or is unable, person by person, to muster the initiative to make it work.

Or an autocratic leader expects that the style that worked fine in the days of being a line supervisor ("Do this. Do that. Now do this.") will work with a team of cross-functional peers. The autocrat quickly finds his orders have no force with the group. Worse, even with all their leader's blustering, the group still needs leadership—articulation of goals, skilled communication, the willingness to teach, and to coordinate.

✔ *Leaders who put themselves ahead of the team.* This is perhaps the most damning indictment of a leader—that the leader has no loyalty to or real identification with the team.

Signs that leaders are only in it for themselves: an unwillingness to run interference for team goals; a disinclination to fight for the team and possibly alienate outside forces; a reluctance to share credit in times of success; a cheerful willingness to point fingers of blame when things go wrong.

Leaders who will not take personal risks for the team are the opposite of leaders. It is doubtful that any initiative can alter their self-serving nature. Confront these leaders and force them to choose between succeeding individually or succeeding as a team.

✔ *Leaders who don't really know the team.* Teams must be committed to one another not just as team members but as people. If I am your team leader and I know your daughter needs an operation, I should want very badly to help you get that operation—as one of the goals of the team.

Some observers go further and say that team members must love one another. That is a hard standard to commit to. Some of us are noticeably unlovable; a few of us head for the hills at the mention of the word *love*. Substitute a phrase with less baggage, however—say that members must *know* and *sympathize with one another as persons*—and the meaning comes into focus.

There are lots of teams that do not "live together"—whose members do not share physical work space, that do not socialize after-hours, that do not eat, breathe, sleep, and dream with the others. Nevertheless there can be no real team, and certainly no leadership, without some degree of intimacy—some human acknowledgment of one another, that we are all people, each one with a unique story, unique difficulties, unique dreams.

Leaders must be the first to make this acknowledgment. Leaders who fail lead teams that are linked by hand, but not by heart. A half-committed team. A team of clock-watchers.

✔ *Inconsistent leaders.* In saying that leadership must exhibit humanity, we open leadership up to all the foibles of human nature. Perhaps the most common of these is inconsistency. Very few people are human ramrods—reliable from day to day, in sun and in shadow—unvarying and mechanical as a streetlight. Leadership has rhythms and contradictions, like any other human behavior. These fluctuations don't cause serious problems in behaviors like walking or snoring; in behaviors like driving a car or leading a team, they do.

It may help to think of this up/down pattern as variation in the classic sense described in the writings of statistician Walter Shewhart[1] and his protege, Wm. Edwards Deming.[2] Without doing violence to the human spirit, variation must be examined and understood, by leader and follower alike.

Ask: What are the causes of these lapses in leadership acuity? Do they appear random and uncontrollable, like the shifting direction of the wind? Is it just natural that we have our good days and our bad days? Or are lapses brought on by predictable and understandable events—fluctuations in personal financial stresses, quota and deadline stress, periodic visits from corporate overseers, with measurement of results?

You may find that stresses cause lapses, or the opposite—that let-downs occur during moments of low accountability or on the heels of a visible success.

The solution: understand and improve those things that can be changed, and stoically accept the things you can't.

✔ *Leaders who cannot be followers.* Most people are members of more than one team. In some team-conscious organizations, an individual may belong to as many as a hundred teams—some lasting

---

[1] Walter A. Shewhart, *Economic Control of Manufactured Product* (Milwaukee: Quality Press), 1980.

[2] Wm. Edwards Deming, *Out of the Crisis* (Cambridge: MIT Press), 1986.

no more than a few minutes—in the course of a work year. So it is inevitable that a leader on one team will be a follower or a peer member on many others.

✔ *Leaders who refuse to acknowledge team members.* One of the first tasks of the leader is enlisting others to follow. Without followership, leadership is something of a moot point. No matter your position, title, or place in the royal birth order, if people aren't willing to follow you, you ain't a leader.

Leaders must see into the hearts and heads of those they would lead. Leaders who think leadership is about them have it exactly wrong. Ignore the team, and the team will ignore you. Acknowledging the contributions of team members (giving credit away), concentrating on recognition, reinforcement, and rewards all go a long way toward solidifying the team leader's legitimacy.

✔ *Leadership that plays favorites.* There is an 80/20 rule in nearly every aspect of organizations: 80 percent of good results come from 20 percent of participants. In the case of customers, it makes good sense to concentrate on attending to the 20 percent that does 80 percent of the business. With team members, however, special treatment prefaces a sudden, steep fall.

Team leaders must walk a tightrope: between knowing each team member individually, knowing what makes that member tick, what motivates him or her, what that member's needs and desires are, and any appearance that one group of team members is more valued than any other. Favoritism is a cancer that eats away at team spirit. For how can a team brandish its musketeer slogan of "All for one and one for all" when leadership is seeing to it that certain musketeers are given a greater ration of gunpowder?

Deming is very firm on this point. Special treatment and merit awards are for the birds, he says. Fawning over individuals—creating a system of team stars and team drones—is one of the surest ways to wreck a team.

✔ *Leaders who do not allow failure.* Teams are melting pots of knowledge and creativity. Their job is twofold: to perform a designated task, and to be continuously improving the way the task is performed. A team can fulfill the first half of that mandate without ever taking chances. No team can fulfill the second half—process improvement—without trying new things. And new things carry a high potential for embarrassment.

Joseph Juran, the Rumanian-born prophet of quality training, calls all mistakes "gold in the mine."[3] What he means is that mistakes are not just mistakes; properly committed, a goof feeds information on what works and what doesn't back into the system. Each failure, so long as it is faced up to and not swept under the carpet, is a golden nugget of information leading a team to greater success.

Some of the most successful teams have created a culture where failure is not only allowed but encouraged—a biweekly prize of $20 for the most egregious screw-up, or the custody of the team trophy until the next noteworthy mishap occurs. This represents a sea change in organizational thinking, of course. Who wants to be known as the first unit in the company to celebrate failure—especially to the folks in finance?

But it is no more radical a change than the move to teams itself. The two principles are, in fact, inseparable. Teams and trial-and-error are both about learning.

If your team leader is uptight about failure, that is again a sign that fear runs the team, and the organization. Leaders must give their teams hope of success by displaying courage in the face of embarrassment. One way to modify the risk and expense of errors is to introduce new ideas on a scaled or pilot basis—on a laboratory basis as opposed to a global, the-whole-world-is-watching basis.

Find ways to overcome, mitigate, or minimize the fear of failure. Then fail your way to success.

✔ *Leaders who protect and blame.* Cannibal organizations—those that, in times of stress, eat their own—have little patience with reports of team screw-ups. The pattern is frightening and predictable: some

---

[3] Joseph A. Juran, ed. *Quality Control Handbook*, Fourth Edition (New York: McGraw-Hill), 1989.

poor devil makes a detectable error, and all around stand, like the stiffs in *Invasion of the Bodysnatchers*, point their fingers and screech.

The useless team leader, as terrified of personal retribution as everyone else, joins in with the pointing and screeching. In such an organization, there may be groups designated as teams. But with people living in such fear, there can be little team feeling or team support.

A good team leader is like a friend, ready to step in and take the occasional bullet. A sane organization cultivates what James Heskett and Earl Sasser[4] call "an atmosphere of blamelessness"—the acknowledgment that bad stuff happens, but that we are all in the business of learning and failing together.

This issue goes so deep, to the heart of a corporation's character, that there is not much that team members can do when its leader betrays them. But team leaders should remind themselves every day of the situation they are in. They have been assigned a difficult task by an organization that will only permit one kind of report—a report that by definition must be a lie. It is a fundamentally dishonest and sadistic situation, one an intelligent individual might risk leaving, for the good of all teams.

✔ *Unethical leaders.* Much has been written about the importance of principles and leadership, but most of it at the executive level. Ethics are important at the team level, as well, especially the ethical tone the team leader sets.

The team does not exist for the leader's sake; quite the opposite. The leader is there to coach team members in skills and teamwork, to assist them with problems they are having in execution, to acknowledge achievement and effort, to share and teach knowledge as it is acquired, to model suitable team behavior, and to periodically remind team members of the team's mission and goals.

These tasks imply above all else a moral simplicity and directness. A leader cannot tell one team member one thing and another team member something quite different. A leader may not ever deceive the

---

[4] James L. Heskett and W. Earl Sasser, Jr., *Breakthrough Service* (New York: The Free Press), 1990.

team. Leaders must not put themselves above the team, for any reason or for any period of time. The leader has been given a trust that is easily violated. For something that happens at work, it is pretty darn sacred.

Does this mean team leaders must behave like St. Francis of the Flowers? No. They should always be themselves. And they should be free to pursue their own ambitions, even if that eventually takes them away from the team. But while they have responsibility for the team they must be true to their role as leaders. And that means continuous improvement of those leadership processes—becoming a better coach, teacher, model, and servant. (For more on trust and teams, see Chapter 15, "Depleted Trust")

✔ *Leaders who are remote.* Conventional leaders may put distance between themselves and those they lead. The distance deliberately limits information followers have. Think of Big Brother in George Orwell's novel *1984*, visible only on telescreens. Or the reclusive movie director. Or baseball manager Connie Mack, who never fraternized, never even dressed in his team's uniform.

The distance was used as a prop. It allowed these leaders to create a cult of personality, of charisma. Take away the distance and people would have seen that Big Brother puts on his pants one leg at a time, that the director is secretly terrified of dealing with people, that 80-year-old manager Connie Mack needed the distance to cover up his impaired faculties.

A true team feeds on information. Leaders who squeeze it through the eye of a needle starve their teams.

✔ *Leaders who fail to model team behavior.* "Do as I say, not as I do." Oh, if only we could get away with that. But we can't. Even kids see through it. Leadership requires mutual respect between team members and leaders. If the team sees you behaving counter to the standards you set as a leader, you'll lose their respect, trust, and followership. Operative term: hypocrisy.

✔ The word *passion* originally meant suffering. The general the soldiers love suffers with them. They have a passion for one another that is real and unstinting. It's OK to talk the talk—provided you first walk the walk.

✔ *Leaders who are oblivious to team members' career needs.* For the entire team to be effective, the needs of individual members must be acknowledged and, when possible, met. Team members do not live to be on the team—they have dreams of moving on to better things some day. When it comes to career development/advancement needs, team leaders are in a much better position to assist because of their role and experience, and because of their knowledge of the internal politics and future needs of the company.

Leaders who actively involve themselves in helping team members achieve career aspirations build trust, loyalty, and comradery.

✔ *Leaders who are unwilling to fight for the team.* The great and paradoxical philosopher Lao Tsu described the role of the true leader as that of a servant. In modern terms, the servant-leader concept translates into the one who establishes the direction (vision, goals, etc.), then runs alongside other team members shouting encouragement, knocking down barriers, opening up networks—running interference. Why would a team fight for a leader who won't fight for them?

✔ *Leaders who are unwilling to take risks.* Ken Melrose, CEO of Toro Co., says leaders must take risks for companies to succeed. Those who take the safe routes tend to get the mediocre results; over time, they are overtaken by competitors. Good leaders encourage calculated (i.e., not *stupid*) risk-taking. If things go wrong, good leaders separate the outcome from the decision—they complain about the outcome, while praising the decision to take the risk in the first place.

Failure, after all, is valuable information. You do not shoot the bringer of such information. Rather, you encourage continued risk-taking, another attempt, a different direction, etc. Leaders who don't encourage their teams to make stretches are rewarded in kind—with unelastic teams.

Two things destroy teams—too little challenge and way, way too much. Find a middle path. Craft challenges that stretch your team, without pulling it apart at the seams.

✔ *Leaders who cannot permit conflict.* We all have a mental picture of the ideal team. Clever people share their ideas, nod appreciatively at one another, and work harmoniously to craft solutions in which everyone participates equally. The picture is the corporate equivalent of a Norman Rockwell—charming, but eerily unreal.

In real life, the lot of the leader is less a Thanksgiving dinner than a combat ration. You present your idea. I sort of listen. As soon as you are done, I lob a pineapple-sized grenade in the vicinity of your flipcharts. We compete. We jostle for advantage. We disagree, sometimes passionately. Often we just don't like each other very much, and the conflict takes on an unpleasant personal edge.

This conflict is very dismaying to many team leaders. They are too smitten by the Norman Rockwell idea, or by their own preconceptions of how teams should behave, or their own innate distaste for disharmony, to endure this very human conflict. We say, there is conflict and there is conflict. Successful teams sometimes behave unattractively, but not dysfunctionally. They do not verbally abuse one another, or sabotage one another's efforts, or pour paint in one another's in-boxes.

Team leaders must expect and must endure the fact that many teams oftentimes more closely resemble kennels than think-tanks. Teams whose leaders are too high-strung or too squeamish or who seek to censor or stifle expression have a problem—the knowledge they must share may not be communicated. They must indicate to the leader that the give-and-take is too valuable to try to "control."

✔ *Leaders who do not value diversity.* Yes, of course—diversity in the sense of equal opportunity for people of races, religious groups, ethnic backgrounds, for both genders, lifestyles, medical conditions and so on. "When in doubt," says diversity guru Jennifer James,[5] "hire the one in the turban." This kind of diversity, on a team dealing with a global and diverse marketplace, is an obvious strength. A leader who is prejudiced against groups belongs in Jurassic Park, not a modern organization. Besides, it's the law.

Looking beyond cave behavior, there is a more important way to think about diversity—as difference. An un-diverse team is a

---

[5] Jennifer James, "When in Doubt, Hire the One in the Turban." (Dallas: The Executive Roundtable), 1994. Audiotape.

white-bread gaggle of yes-men—often quite literally. A truly diverse team brings together not just people with different backgrounds but different ways of thinking.

To be valuable to the organization, diversity has to go way beyond legal compliance to an opportunistic cherry-picking of team members for the different outlooks—different knowledge and ideas—each member can bring to the table. A great team is one without factions, because no one is in automatic, cultural agreement with anyone else.

A great team leader is one who can not only live with this differentness but can revel in the clash of values, exult in disagreement, and honor the spirit of dissent. Hint: Team leaders don't have to be white males just because they have always been.

✔ *Leaders who are passive.* Think of leadership as a set of *initiating activities.* It is about moving things—a product, a service, an idea, a team—from here to there.

Where managers are properly reactive, responding with existing knowledge to existing circumstances, leaders must be proactive, acquiring and teaching new knowledge for contiunously changing circumstances. Managers mostly stay in place; leaders are on the move.

Leadership is not better than managership. You can't vault over one to get to the other. Think of management—knowing when and how to react appropriately—as a foundation for leadership. Once the foundation is firmly in place, leadership takes over. Then you must build skills and confidence to take initiative and risk to move the team forward.

You may be a good manager (reactive, firefighting) but not a good leader (proactive, planning). But you cannot be a great leader without first being, at the very least, a decent manager.

What a leader must do to get people to follow

First, don't head toward any cliffs. Second, the leader must follow, by knowing what people's needs are, and helping to meet them. A starving army cannot fight. A frustrated workforce cannot compete.

When our crystal ball clouds over and we forget what leadership is, we set aside abstract considerations and focus on folks like Ted H. and Jim S. They are the distilled essence of what team leading is about. Having said that, Ted and Jim are not all that unique. They are like many of the team leaders we have encountered in our travels within, without, up, down, and through organizations. We all read the magazine articles heralding the senior executive heroes who lead their organizations to the promised land. For our money, there are thousands more leaders, at the operating (management) and front-line (supervisory) levels, who have made those top managers successful by continually challenging the status quo and unfailingly pursuing quality and performance improvement.

Their contributions as team leaders add up to much more than a day's work for a day's pay. They are the points of origin for those small, project-by-project, performance breakthroughs that hone their organization's competitive edge to razor sharpness. Their efforts reliably produce a bigger bang for the buck, essentially *adding value* to their organizations through distinctive team leadership activity. From this, we propose a working definition of a team leader:

Team leaders add value by leveraging their organizations' assets and outcomes beyond expectations. The result of this value-adding leadership is enhanced performance in four different dimensions:

- self and others
- awareness and choice
- focus and integration
- innovation and action taking

What does adding value mean in the context of team leadership? Leaders add value by getting more than required or expected out of what they have to work with—existing human and physical resources. Working cooperatively with other people, they appear to successfully guide problem solving, fix things, innovate, and capture opportunity more often and at a faster pace than many of their peers.

Are we saying team leaders are inherently supermen or superwomen, freakish examples of inborn leaderly genius? No. Rather, that today's top team leaders do whatever they need to do to:

1. perform at a very high level of competence and productivity themselves, and

2. educe solid effort and performance from the people they work with

Let us underscore that we are talking mostly about everyday operating managers and front-line supervisors down in the trenches. We are not talking about the executive nameplates on mahogany row.

What team leaders do

Team leaders leverage *self* and *others*. First, they leverage high levels of performance from themselves. Then, as surely as the night follows the day, they leverage a similar level of performance from the people they work with. An alternative name for a good team leader might be "quiet revolutionary." The best are infectious self-starters like Jim and Ted, who cannot help but positively influence others around them.

By leveraging themselves and others, team leaders:

☛ **Project energy.** They provide task excitement, motivation, spirit. Depending on their personalities they can be as quiet and unassuming as woodchucks. Or they can be all over the place, raucous, chattering, in your face. Whatever their personalities, the leaders we have known have all been *activists*, catalysts for positive action, never happy on the sidelines. In particular, they seem to take care to avoid the negative, declining to join in at the periodic bitch sessions enumerating the many reasons "you can't get there from here." Instead they take the road less traveled, opting to encourage others and, with everyone participating, piecing together solutions to the problems of the day.

☛ **Are involved, involving, and empowering of others.** Without being obtrusive, they walk around, nudging, assisting, helping, asking questions. They put out and they bring in—they share information they have and they build others into new work processes and projects. The result of all this busy-ness is a greater sense of involvement all around. Good leaders recognize that involvement is not an abstract theoretical point—it's something that you live and breathe on the job, and it requires continual practice. Leaders not only involve others; we have often observed them sharing whatever power, influence, and other resources they have with other team members. Here comes the dread word . . . they *empower* others to get the job done willingly, rapidly, and well. Leaders appear unconcerned about losing control or sharing power; trading these slight risks for the improved motivation and performance flowing from their empowering efforts.

☛ **Assist evolution and change.** Guiding, smoothing, and helping others map out and explore the pathways of opportunity. In today's churning organizational environment, this ability to evolve and change is absolutely key to survival. But it's rough—change invokes our fear of the unknown and threatens our habits and previous momentum. Our natural response to the need to change is *resistance*. Leaders understand that foot-dragging is part of the change process. Instead of bulldozing ahead, riding up and over the bodies and minds of those resisting, good team leaders plan ahead, involving others early on and communicating what's happening and why to all concerned. Perhaps most important, they help others realistically appreciate what's in it for them. When fear of the unknown is the ailment, knowledge and communication are the medicine. The great leader banishes fear and replaces it with hope of success.

☛ **Persuade and persevere.** Good leaders identify obstacles, then take them out, blocking and tackling to create running room for the team. Instead of knocking people on their backsides, however, they clear the path by winning over those who stand in the way. We can scarcely contain our amazement sometimes as we have watched (or experienced) the different approaches good leaders take to advance team goals. Some come straight at you, insisting on your support and any resources you can provide. Others employ more subtle strategies: bargaining, trading, exchanging, showing the obvious benefits, using third-party advocates, etc. As with Ted H., many have little positional power; they instead find support from those who do. This task requires skill. It also requires the tenacity of a terrier. They identify a valued outcome, grab it like the leg of your trousers, and simply keep shaking. They persevere. And their persistence is of such a quality that people are turned not off but on.

◦○◦

Team leaders leverage *awareness* and *choice*. Organizations succeed when people within those organizations are aware of the problems and/or opportunities. That sounds elementary, but in reality, there are zillions of outfits where the philosophy is "ready, shoot, aim"—where workers go through the motions of performing their tasks without framing in their own minds what issues are at stake, or what alternative actions might be taken. Without understanding, people just do what has always been done—often to everyone's later regret. Good team leaders are people of action—but only after they have pushed for reasoned insight, heightened awareness, and thoughtful choice.

By leveraging awareness and choice, team leaders:

☛ **Look beyond the obvious.** Human organizations are not anthills, where instinct is the best bulwark against destruction; we need to think things through. Team leaders value the search for information and the best feasible choice among alternatives. Successful "hipshooters" are rare among team leaders. Team leaders spend time up front, finding out what questions to ask, analyzing situations, and most especially seeking to involve the people who will play a part of any implementation. Often, their inquiry is informal, relying on those with the most relevant experience. Many leaders, however, have no reluctance to take the time, expense, and effort of using more sophisticated techniques. They seem to take inordinate pride in doing quality work the first time and avoiding the distressing necessity of "engineering in the field" later.

☛ **Maintain perspective.** Lose the big picture on any team, its overarching vision, and goals, and you lose everything. Leaders keep their eyes on the prize, and they foster a "systems view" to guide analysis and action. Team leaders gather a lot of initial and ongoing information. This not only helps team members to understand the processes they are engaged in, but it helps avoid myopic tunnel vision and dedication to a single course of action. Leaders appear sensitive to the impact of recommendations and changes they propose (or undertake) on other parts of the organization. They tend to ask a lot of what-if questions up front, seeking to avoid unintended consequences. Their willingness to consider the organization as a "connected system" not only limits the firing of loose cannons, but it pays off in fostering cooperation from other leaders who worry less about the chaos generated when the cannon balls hit.

Pyramid learning. We have found team leaders to be habitual teachers. They stress the need to understand a situation and the options available and assist others to explore and appreciate the possibilities. They not only investigate and take action, but they seem to hook those around them on the need to absorb what is happening and why. This openness to learning explains one of the greatest things about good leaders—they are not completely irreplaceable, because they have opened so many other people up to knowledge and the spirit of inquiry.

○○○

Team leaders leverage *focus* and *integration*. Focus being a team's ability to fix its attention on a goal or task, and integration being individual team members' ability to "get with the program." Consider what happens when neither is leveraged. Too often in our work with organizations we have noticed a pair of sad but distinct phenomena: one we call the "spaghetti toss" and the other going by the nickname "turf honcho." In the first case, the organization abounds with unfocused activity and project work—much of it never contributing to overall success. It is as if the organization, not knowing any better, was tossing spaghetti on the wall to see what sticks. In the second case, how many times is the wheel reinvented or something drops through organizational cracks because of someone's need to put boundaries up and manage their turf?

In sharp contrast, team leaders maximize their team's focus and integration. Thus they:

☛ **Target energy on success opportunities.** We have all experienced the problem of too much opportunity and not enough direction. Success opportunities don't arrive with little maps telling you where the treasure is buried. You have to figure that out yourself. Each new path forks off in a dozen different ways. Effective leaders assist team members and others in choosing the right paths and setting the right priorities. Together they focus their efforts toward high-promise activities and outcomes. We have observed team leaders working with others in some very collaborative ways, across all kinds of organization boundaries, to test alternatives and get a bearing on the most promising courses of action. Once this focus is achieved, it is as if a red light has switched on for the duration of the project. Teams are able to extend the cooperative spirit generated during these cross-unit, cross-function, cross-level analyses into any later implementation process.

☛ **Foster task linkage with others.** Most of us live in "functional cages" labeled Marketing, Personnel, Finance, Operations, etc. Within these cages or silos we toil in even smaller groups on all the tasks necessary to organizational success. From this narrow perspective, we rarely see and comprehend the size and shape of the elephant entrusted to our care. Effective team leaders break down the cages and expand people's way of seeing, beyond their narrow task. They create a common bond with other teams and a sense of shared fate and opportunity. Team leaders spend lots and lots of time working across boundaries. They help folks feel "we are in this together." With the help of other team members and other teams we can get this elephant on its feet and moving in the proper direction.

☛ **Influence cooperative action.** Creating linkage isn't enough. Leaders have to go beyond that and engender a true climate for cooperation. Effective leaders turn fences into bridges. This is not an easy task—cooperative action-taking requires lots of set-up and tons of follow-through. Neither of us could begin to count the number of times we have experienced or observed failure in organizations because individuals or units simply could not cooperate. There are many reasons for this kind of "dis-cooperation." Some people see no great need for cooperation, and they never bother to develop the requisite skills to carry it off. Others fear sharing credit with the next unit. Many shut out others until the last moment, when it's too late to elicit genuine cooperation. So it goes. Whatever the reason, we have often found team leaders purposely building relationships across organizational boundaries *pre-need* (that phrase comes courtesy of the mortuary profession). *Note:* Team leaders actively identify and influence those who have access to resources necessary to the tasks they undertake. Thus cooperation is planned and designed into every task. *Note also:* Sensible team leaders rarely burn their bridges to others, no matter what the provocation. Future cooperation is too important to throw away in a moment of emotional indulgence.

o O o

Team leaders leverage *innovation* and *performance*. You read about business heroes out there, creating incredible advancements, engineering impossible accomplishments. Nice work, if you can do it. Those we would tag as team leaders are more often ordinary folks who generate improvement bit by bit, consuming our poor, much discussed elephant one bite at a time.

To leverage innovation and performance, they:

☞ **Support creativity.** They challenge team members to invest their time, talent, and resources in the quest. Here, we aren't talking about innovative product creation, support for much ballyhooed skunkworks, etc. Rather, what team leaders seem to value highly are creative approaches to perceived problems or some new twist that captures an opportunity. Team leaders are more than just tinkerers— always adjusting, trying out, testing, etc. Ted, for example, is absolutely unrelentingly in the quest for small technical or procedural innovations to produce a better baggage handling process in service to what he sees as "his passengers."

☞ **Take initiative.** Team leaders at all levels will seize initiative. Great leaders are great doers, catalysts who can take what-if thinking and galvanize it into action. They take reasonable risks and encourage others to do likewise and to invest their resources to improve the way their organizations work. Our experience suggests that team leaders quickly size up an improvement opportunity, involve others, come up with a plan, and then simply get on with it. In the course of our discussions, another interesting facet of their initiative-taking behavior cropped up: "I'd rather ask for forgiveness than permission," was the express comment made by several team leaders when asked to sum up their approach to getting things done. As the Nike commercial says, "Just do it."

☛ **Eschew the negative.** I.e., they accentuate the positive. Team leaders continually challenge themselves and their team members to maintain a work environment where people are glad to participate. This often means creating a "service environment" in the workplace—whether the organization delivers a conventional service or not—and setting high standards of quality and service to customers both inside and out. We were struck by the recent comment of a retail supervisor whom we immediately tagged as a team leader. Discussing motivation she exclaimed: "You know, you can whip the 'slaves' and make them work, but you can't make them serve one another, or the paying customer, that way." The comment put words to our overall sense that team leaders generally seek to create a positive work environment. This fits with our view, that a punitive work setting results in CYA (Cover-Your-Anterior) team leadership—the exact opposite of what effective team leaders model.

Our experience suggests that folks who feel punitively treated spend their energies grousing about their troubles, "getting even," pursuing outside interests, etc.—and not looking for ways to improve quality or provide service to their colleagues or customers. Team leaders, in sharp contrast, appear to do three things. First, they model and coach positive interaction with others. Second, they either help to get rid of punitive rules and practices or buffer their people from their effects where possible. And third, if you mutter about "how bad it is" within earshot of them, you'll be gently given the opportunity to help make it better.

☛ **Are never satisfied.** The spirit of team leadership is one of continuous improvement. A good leader can never be convinced that existing structures, processes, and outcomes are as good as they could or should be. Again, this shouldn't come as a big surprise. What's important to note, however, is *how* they go about the process. Incremental change—transforming a team one day at a time, one bit at a time—is still a team leader's best strategy for effecting systematic improvement. In part, this approach is forced on them by their positions, often well down in the bowels of the organizational pyramid, with limited positional power or material resources. In part, it seems a strategy of choice. One team leader confided: "Even the biggest improvements I've been a part of happened one small project at a time. Plus, I always feel a sense of accomplishment when I get to see some results early." We see a clear and obvious second element to their improvement strategy.

○○○

Throughout this chapter we have highlighted team leaders involving others, early and often. In so doing, they leverage their own efforts while focusing the skills and cooperative action necessary to tackle "cross-boundary" problems and opportunities.

If your team is having difficulties, the odds of leadership being at the root of the difficulties is very high. You, too must find a path between the old and the new, to find what works for your group. Because "what works" is the very heart and soul of good team leadership. Keep trying things, like Edison and his incandescent bulb, until something lights up.

chapter 11

·

faulty vision

·

if you don't know where you're going
. . . you'll probably get there

I've got good news and bad.
The bad news is that we're lost.
The good news is that we're making great time.

The point of this old saw is that team talent, efficiency, intelligence, and clout are pretty doggone useless unless the team has some clue where it's going and how it's to contribute to the organization's overall strategies for success.

We're talking about vision here, one of the most misunderstood and misapplied ideas making the rounds now. Vision is not a "vision statement." It is not something created in hindsight or with an eye toward external consumption. It is not something you pay consultants $250 per hour to create for you at a weekend retreat. It does not exist on a report to shareholders or in a guarantee to customers. It is not really words. It is a burning thought, and it exists only in the heads (and hearts) of the team.

The vision is the thing the team exists to do, defined in ambitious form. It is the thing that leadership makes happen. Without team vision, there is no point to a team.

Vision begins at the corporate level, setting the course for the enterprise as a whole. With the help of leadership it trickles down, uniting the subunits of the enterprise, helping them figure out their role in the bigger picture.

The most common vision problem teams have is one that is fundamentally beyond their control: the team has a vision, but the enterprise doesn't. It's a sad thing, but no amount of ambition, intelligence, and hard work at the trench level can succeed if the vision of the organization as a whole is a drag. "Returning the greatest possible return on investment to our shareholders" is the best-known offender.

Getting the picture

Vision is the offspring of hunger. Companies that have succeeded in the past and that had a vision in the past may think the old vision is still in effect. But in many cases it is gone, rubbed clean by the passage of time, complacency in high places, and the high-gloss buffing of corporate communications types.

It is not until a company hits hard times, some rude awakening of the marketplace, that it learns it must have a clue why it is in business. This is a perilous moment. Companies in peril, sensing they need to stand for something, have a tendency to try to stand for a lot of different things in rapid succession. The resulting wheel-spinning, drum-beating, and horn-blowing can be devastating to that organization's teams. They are like fish in a blender, doing their best against woeful odds.

Having a clearly communicated vision, on the other hand, allows employees and team members to measure their values and behaviors against a company standard. If there is a value clash, people are free to either modify their values or leave. Teams are better off when some people leave—not that they are deadwood, but because their resistance to the vision of the team had to have a drag on productivity and morale.

Pitfalls of communicating the vision

It is the role of corporate leadership to excite senior management about the corporate vision. It is the role of the team leader or leaders to keep the vision alive at the team level. It is a slippery task. It requires communication, but it requires more than that. It requires exhortation, just a little (a little exhortation goes a long way). It requires nagging, in a way—badgering people with the vision a dozen times a day, keeping it in their face, whatever is necessary to keep that idea obvious and up front for everyone.

More than these things, it requires magic: taking an idea that is in your head and subtly and artfully remaking it in every head on the team. Like the sower and the seed, the leader plants and nourishes the idea, keeps it alive, and allows team members to understand, each one in his or her own way, why it is advantageous, desirable, and achievable. Team leaders can easily fail in this magical task. Here are some of the standard pitfalls:

☛ **Assigning.** Too often, leaders seek to assign the vision. This is what it is, they say. Here are descriptions. Memorize and replicate! It's not a bad way to spread the word, provided everyone on the team is a clone of the leader.

☛ **Dullness.** Leaders whose pilot lights have blown out are not likely to light many fires under team members. Vision is a must—emotion is a natural part of creating and communicating it. This is not something leaders can turn on or off, like hydraulic fluid. It must be genuine.

☛ **Waffling.** Leaders cannot experiment, explaining the idea one way to one subgroup and another way to another subgroup. Leaders cannot learn the vision as they preach it. If it is some sort of moving, evolving target, everyone will miss it.

☛ **Selling.** Another failure is when the leader, often charged up by some consultant or author, tries to replicate the process with himself or herself playing the role of consultant, essentially selling the idea to others. It's a bad role, because it positions the leader as outsider. Better to use the natural leverage of a trusted insider and to hold off on the soft soap.

☑ **Nonaligning.** The proper way to spread a vision is to work with people as individuals to bring their wants and needs into alignment with the team vision. Treat everyone equally. No arm-twisting, wheedling, or cajolery. Show people the respect they deserve as adults and as members of your team, and they will treat your idea with the same respect. You cannot own it for them; they must come to own the idea . . . on their own.

chapter 12

·

toxic teaming atmosphere

·

organizational karma

Teams make themselves over time. Outsiders can institute or create them, stock them and roll-call them. A team is not a team until the team agrees it is a team. Even so, no team can thrive in an environment that is hostile to teamwork. The most egregious toxins in team atmosphere are *competition, tyranny,* and assorted forms of team foolishness, including *mob behavior.* All can easily occur within a team, and they do so frequently. They are most hazardous, however, when imposed from without.

We seek here to show how to move from team competition to team collaboration; how to avoid team tyranny; how to be wise about when to team and when to not team; and the characteristics of effective team members.

Competition most foul

Several years ago, Harvey was working in a small division of a much larger company that had morale problems, and he couldn't quite figure out what was going wrong. After poking around, he discovered the general manager of the division gained sadistic pleasure from watching his teams compete and scramble with each other for limited resources and few rewards.

While interviewing team resource folks, Harvey also discovered that resources weren't nearly as scarce as had been broadcast by the GM. This gentleman simply thought "putting the squeeze on" would heighten the level of team competition. He was right. The resulting friction between teams eventually raised the temperature within teams to the point of team meltdown. The resulting toll on division morale was evident to everyone—except you-know-who.

What we say about this may violate your deeply held principles, but hear us out:

> *There is no such thing*
> *as friendly competition.*
> *Especially on teams.*

Competition, the way people usually mean the word, is essentially a win/lose proposition. The competitor who wins gets the gravy today, but the competitor who loses is going to try to get even tomorrow.

Teaming is more of a collaborative effort. Collaboration assumes that all sides can win, not on every point of every agenda, but enough of a win on the important points that staying together as a team remains mutually reinforcing and profitable to all.

Competitors are opponents, withholding information from one another. Collaborators are colleagues who share rather than hoard, rely on one another's experience and expertise to support team outcomes—and advance individual goals.

Teams collaborate within themselves to succeed, and they continue to collaborate with other teams, linking arms to achieve the outcomes of the enterprise. Pitting teams against one another ("Team Red," "Team Blue," etc.), with rewards and recognition going to the team that leaves the others behind is just that—the pits.

Bottom-line thinking alone should tell you that interteam competition is a bad idea. It promotes the exact opposite results that teams are capable of achieving. Instead of optimizing resources, you waste the efforts and goodwill of the teams coming in second.

Toxic teaming atmosphere is not always of the organization's making. Individuals and groups within the team have plenty of power to shape the teaming climate. As a young journalist, Mike went from a news office whose team leader was confident, open, and comfortable to a newsroom where the leader had disappeared into a glass booth. Where the first newsroom was a place of comradery, laughter, and genuine affection, the second was a place of insecurity, striving, and jockeying for survival.

Had management been aware that the team was devouring itself day by day, it might conceivably have stepped in and put things right. But, as so often is the case with teams, management doesn't always give a hoot—and the troubled team is left to stew in its own juices.

Team tyranny

Team tyranny is the heavy hand of the organization at large, forcing everyone to do everything on a team basis. The logic is underwhelming: "Teams are great, so—let's insist everything be done that way."

As an example, let's pick on one of our favorite companies, Honeywell. On the plus side, Honeywell has a long tradition of idea leadership. On the minus side, this appetite for new ideas has occasionally meant getting carried away with organizational fads. A new word gains currency (*quality, reengineering*, etc.), and people lose their minds.

In the late 1970s and early '80s, when quality circles were just catching on in American corporations, Honeywell plunged deeper into the idea than most. Honeywell's corporate human resources people began modestly with six well-trained circles. Soon, every executive and manager wanted circles to call their own, and they formed them, without coordinating or training them in any noticeable way. Within six months, the company had 625 down-and-dirty quality circles.

Now, we know what happened to quality circles nationwide—they failed, because they had no power and no one listened to them. The chaos, confusion, disenchantment, anger, etc., at Honeywell was enormous. Within 18 months, 620 of these teams died miserable deaths with QC residue left on everyone's hands.

Given that experience, it is no wonder companies like Honeywell are fighting uphill battles implementing total quality management and other team-oriented programs today. All they have to do is look at their hands and remember: *Quality* did this to us.

Well, it's still happening. The only thing that has changed is the word. This time it's *teaming*. Be on a team or lose steam. What sort of person could object to such a good idea as teaming? Well, any kind of person could, if it makes no sense. Most people, when asked, would say teamwork is good and they probably are on a team or two. The problems arise when teamwork is made mandatory and people feel pressured to form teams for everything.

Team tyranny ("You *must* be democratic, you *must* be open, you *must* share!") sounds ironic and unlikely. But it happens all the time. If you see it happening, make it stop.

Teams vs. mobs

In the rush to bestow the manifold blessings of teams upon our organizations, lots of things get called teams that probably shouldn't be. The resulting groups are too big, too lumpy, mismatched, and more than a little confused.

We call these assemblages mobs. There are ways to differentiate real teams from fake teams or mobs (see chart on page 111).

So, how do you keep from creating mobs instead of teams?

First of all, sort team membership into two categories: *core team* members and *resource team* members. Core team members are on a project from start to finish with close to 100 percent of their time and priorities dedicated to the project's outcomes. Resource team members, by contrast, are members of project teams on an as-needed basis. They are just as valuable as core team members but are only involved with the team as their expertise and input are required.

A resource team member is more likely, therefore, to be on several teams at any one time. Resource team members may sometimes be asked to participate from the beginning of a project to minimize their learning curve once they become more active in the team's discussions.

Wise teams use these resource team members, who are always just a phone call away, not just as "seagulls" who swoop in as needed to drop

TEAMS	vs.	MOBS

TEAMS	MOBS
Members recognize their interdependence and understand both personal and team goals are best accomplished with mutual support. Time is not wasted struggling over turf or attempting personal gain at the expense of others.	Members think they are grouped together for administrative purposes only. Individuals work independently; sometimes at cross purposes with others.
Members feel a sense of ownership for their jobs and unit because they are committed to goals they helped establish.	Members tend to focus on themselves because they are not sufficiently involved in planning the unit's objectives. They approach their job simply as a hired hand.
Members contribute to the organization's success by applying their unique talent and knowledge to team objectives.	Members are told what to do rather than being asked what the best approach would be. Suggestions are not encouraged.
Members work in a climate of trust and are encouraged to openly express ideas, opinions, disagreements and feelings. Questions are welcomed.	Members distrust the motives of colleagues because they do not understand the role of others members. Expressions of opinion or disagreement are considered divisive or non-supportive.
Members practice open and honest communication. They make an effort to understand each other's point of view.	Members are so cautious about what they say that real understanding is not possible. Game playing may occur and communications traps may be set to catch the unwary.
Members are encouraged to develop skills and apply what they learn on the job. They receive the support of the team.	Members may receive good training but are limited in applying it to the job by the supervisor or other group members.
Members recognize conflict as a normal aspect of human interaction but they view such situations as an opportunity for new ideas and creativity. They work to confront and resolve conflict quickly and constructively.	Members find themselves in conflict situations which they do not know how to resolve. They do not differentiate confrontation and conflict. Their supervisor or "team leader" may put off intervention until serious damage is done.
Members participate in decisions affecting the team, but understand their leader must make a final ruling whenever the team cannot decide, or an emergency exists. Positive results, not conformity, is the goal.	Members may or may not participate in decisions affecting the team. Conformity often appears more important than positive results.

their load and take off again, but as valued team members who, over the life of a project, can contribute much more than just an allotment of expertise.

Consultants as resource team members

Team consulting is one of the growth industries of the 1990s. Consultants are often part of the initial impetus to switch to team-based work. As teams splatter into brick walls, these same people are often there, brimming with I-told-you-so's and bullet-point solutions.

These are not bad people. In fact, they are important players in the effort to transform organizations from the scientific-management, pyramid-style, bureaucratic paradigm of the old days to the more efficient, more participative team approach of today. If you think of an organization as a living body, a good consultant is like Vitamin C—an outside catalyst for positive change.

The challenge with consultants is to get your money's worth from them. This means lengthening the utility of their good initial message from the typical 72-hour euphoria period, in which everyone on the team suddenly "gets it" and can envision an idea taking hold and recreating team processes and attitudes, to the let-down period that so typically follows.

The first thing you must do with consultants is get them to admit that they are consultants and helpless in the face of the need to keep consulting. When pushed, most will make this concession. Here are some other measures teams can take to keep good ideas alive.

☑ **Talk the idea up.** Team members shouldn't meet with the consultant "cold." Let the team know in advance that the topic is important, that it won't be filed away as so many good ideas are. Both before and after the presentation, publicize and explain it. Maybe corporate or divisional internal communications staff can get involved. Afterwards, ask the employee newsletter to devote a page listing and recognizing worker suggestions. Have the team sponsor attend, and invite him or her to comment on how the idea might be adapted to the team.

☛ **Summarize the key points and post them conspicuously.** Bulletin boards are great. E-mail roundtables work great, too. Even better is to post simple, memorable material on the walls of the team work space.

☛ **Plan follow-up meetings to discuss implementation.** Have the team meet over coffee. Explain to non-attendees what the message was. Ask people what will be the implications of implementing the kinds of cycle time (or whatever) improvements the consultant suggested. What will need to be changed for the new approach to succeed?

☛ **Be patient.** Old dogs can learn new tricks, but it may take a while. Allow for missteps and confusion. The usual expectations will probably have to be modified.

☛ **Return to the source.** No rule says you can't call the consultant back for a clarification—even a year later. They can show you where you went wrong and how to get back on track. If the consultant is too busy, or too expensive, find secondary sources— books, magazines, or a consultant who does have time for you.

☛ **Anticipate resistance.** Negative-minded people are relieved when initiatives disintegrate; positive-minded people, by contrast, must bypass the negativism of others to make any headway. The challenge to team leaders is to make the best use of both attitudes—the positive to be open to and explore new ideas; the negative to analyze and critique them.

☛ **Change the mindset.** Team leaders must cultivate an open-minded working atmosphere where new ideas are not dismissed out of hand, where a few negative personalities effectively censor events before they have a chance to occur.

☛ **Maintain a balance.** Don't be like the kid with the new drum who forgets all his other toys. If improving cycle time (or whatever) becomes an obsession, team members will switch you and your enthusiasm off. A balanced approach, which recognizes the difficulties of implementing a new idea within an existing framework, has the best chance of success.

When to team

If you are *absolutely sure* that a team is what you need, then you must map the team out. This means deciding who the right core and resource team members are, actually forming the team, and following the pathway outlined in Chapter 22.

Even at this stage it's still not too late to give up on the team approach. You don't need teams when:

- decisions are best made by one person
- decisions are predetermined
- the outcome is not critical to company, division, department success (like what color toilet paper to buy)
- time is of the essence (a decision by tomorrow)
- the project is either "back burner" or a low priority

Teams are best used when they are formed to address short-term, high priority, perhaps cross-functional, single-focused, action-oriented outcomes. You need teams when:

- the wider the input the better the output
- the issue is cross-functional or multi-directional in nature
- the outcome/decision has potential high-impact for department, division, or company

Don't feel pressured to form a team because it's the thing to do now. If it doesn't feel right, the heck with it. Form teams only when they *make sense* and the team output will be greater than the sum of the individual members' inputs.

The team biosphere

How do you create a great team atmosphere? First ask, whose job is it to do this?

It is *everyone's* responsibility to create the teaming atmosphere, by fulfilling their roles within the team. We use the phrase *organizational karma* to describe this shared responsibility for climate control. Karma being the wheel of consequences, with good deeds and bad deeds alike coming back to us continually. We could as easily use an expression from software development: GIGO—"Garbage in, garbage out." Or as they say in the submarines, when you are all breathing the same air, forgo that second helping of beans.

Here they are, the characteristics of effective team members:

☛ **Having a commitment to goals.** It is difficult to work enthusiastically toward an outcome if you don't know what that outcome is. The first thing good team members do is clarify what they're after—what their team goals and objectives are. With this clarified, good team members commit themselves to the outcome; whatever it takes (within ethical boundaries), they are willing to do.

☛ **Showing a genuine interest in other team members.** People don't have to like each other to work together. That may be true, in the short term. But good team members develop a genuine interest in the well-being of other team members. Not as a team survival mechanism, but as a human bond. It may sound like small talk, but it's more caring: "How was your weekend?" "Is your child still sick?" "Is there anything I can do?"

☛ **Confronting conflict.** Good team members can tell the difference between confrontation and conflict—between directness and having a chip on one's shoulder. The only way to discover and resolve differences within the team is to open up, acknowledge the disagreement, and negotiate a solution. Avoid the plague, but own up to conflict. As a matter of fact, effective team members intercede when other team members are in conflict, to help resolve the disagreement. Bad or weak team members turn their back on conflict and either ignore it, and hope it will disappear, or let the other team members battle it out, squandering precious team time and goodwill.

☛ **Listening empathically.** Empathic, active listening is important for anyone, whether you're on a team or not. It is particularly important for open communication between effective team members. Empathic listening means being sensitive to not just the content of the message the other person is sending but to the emotion behind the message. Good listening means more than shutting up and waiting for your turn—it means getting into the other person's head and heart.

☛ **Practicing inclusive decision making.** Good team members run their "first draft" decision by other team members before they pull the trigger. One never knows what additional inputs you may acquire that may make your tentative decision even better. Not only may you get additional information this way, but you have a communication device online that lets people know where your thoughts are headed—thus minimizing surprises later.

☛ **Valuing individual differences.** Effective team members look at differences as positive. They respect the opinions of others and view other's perspectives as pluses, not minuses. They figure out how to use the natural differences to benefit the team's outcomes and not as excuses to avoid working with each other.

☛ **Contributing ideas freely.** Good team members don't hold back their ideas. When they have an opinion about something, they express it, even if it's just to support someone else's opinion. If you have an idea about the topic being discussed and you keep your mouth shut (very typical for the Midwest, where we are), you're not being an effective team member.

☛ **Providing feedback on team performance.** Good teams develop a method for providing continuous feedback on how the team is working, what's going right, what's going wrong, and what to do about it. Effective team members also solicit feedback from other team members ("How'm I doing?"). No matter what formal performance feedback system their organizations provide, good teams develop methods for more frequent, real-time, relevant feedback on people, processes, team support structures, and outcomes.

☑ **Celebrating accomplishments.** One of the first questions Harvey asks when doing teaming within an organization is, "When was the last time you folks had a party?" If you haven't had a party lately, you haven't had a formal excuse to celebrate. Maybe your goals are long term ones; it's hard to break off in the middle and celebrate. So—do it anyway. Effective teams find excuses to celebrate, usually related to the accomplishment of some shorter term outcome. Look for ways to lift the morale through celebration, both personal and professional.

chapter 13

•

communication shortfalls

•

how'm i doing?

Your company is insisting it wants great teamwork. Everywhere you look, it's team this and team that. Employees get the message loud and clear. But that's the only message they get.

Once they "team," they feel like they have climbed a tall tree, to the highest branches, and as far as they can see, there's nothing. No mail trucks, no telephone lines, no smoke signals. They're literally up in a tree, left to their own devices, blinking. Even if you create a team with a magic wand, it must be sustained the old-fashioned way, with lots of TLC—Teaching, Learning, and Communication.

Teaching, learning, and communication

A team, before it is anything else, is about knowledge. How to get it, how to improve it, and how to pass it on. In the old days knowledge was a byproduct of doing business; today it is a primary driver. The distinctions between working and learning have never been blurrier.

If you look up and down our "Why Teams Go Wrong" matrix in Chapter 1, you will see that every dysfunction a team can slip into (poor leadership, ill-defined goals, personality struggles, etc.) are really failures of learning. Leaders paying attention to their leading, and listening to those they are leading, should learn their way toward better leadership.

Teams that have struggled with ambiguous objectives in the past should have learned the knack for identifying a fuzzy objective in the present and be able to discuss among themselves how to bring it into sharper focus. Team members who have gone up in flames doing battle with one another for reasons having to do with one another's personalities must learn the futility of infighting and intolerance and develop the skills for better appreciating one another (or at least not going at one another with chainsaws).

If we are not learning from past experience, it is probably because we are not sharing what we have learned with one another. This is the paradox of communication—that so often we all know the right answer to a question, but for a variety of reasons we decide to keep our mouths shut about it.

A wonderful and influential article about this very paradox appeared many years ago in *Organizational Dynamics* magazine. It was called "The Abilene Paradox: The Management of Agreement," by Jerry B. Harvey.[1] He starts by citing an absurd outing his own family went on one very hot day down in Texas. The family was sitting comfortably at home when the father-in-law suddenly said, "Let's get in the car and go to Abilene and have dinner at the cafeteria."

When polled, every family member said that sounded like a good idea. So they piled into the car and drove the 106 miles in 104-degree heat to Abilene. Once in Abilene, the conspiracy of cheerfulness dissipated. Everyone wanted to know whose idea the trip was. "I just went along to be nice," some said. "I went along because you went along."

Jerry Harvey realized he had stumbled on an important rule of behavior—that people can miscommunicate just as badly out of good intentions as out of bad. How many times have you happily consented to do something you didn't want to do, in order to be a "team player"? A team worth its salt would shudder at that behavior passing itself off

---

[1] Jerry B. Harvey, "The Abilene Paradox: The Management of Agreement." *Organizational Dynamics,* Summer 1974, pp. 63–80.

as team behavior. It is a form of laziness and cowardice—and one every team has to stand watch against.

Communication horror stories

How important is communication? Here are two horror stories from this morning's (it is September 1994 on your earth calendar) newspaper:

The National Reconnaissance Office, or NRO, is in a heap of trouble. They are one of those secret government organizations you never hear about, yet here they are, getting heard about. Seems they went and built a 1-million-square-foot, $350-million office complex right next to Dulles International Airport in Washington, DC. Problem was, no one seemed to know about it. Congress claimed to have no knowledge of it. It wasn't a line item in the budget everyone battled over. The CIA, which is supposed to run the NRO, didn't have a clue. The President, who is supposed to know everything, didn't know nothin'. The top NRO official insisted he had told (in bits and pieces) a select group of individuals in Congress, and they were supposed to pass the word to other Congress people. But the select few didn't communicate with each other to put the puzzle together. Congress couldn't be trusted to know about this, hush-hush stuff, etc. If these elected officials had communicated what they knew, what they were supposed to communicate with each other, they wouldn't have ended up with egg on their faces. It was a classic case of the government not trusting itself—thus making itself less trustworthy to us, the people.

oOo

In the middle of the night, a radar screen at the Federal Aviation Authority picks up a single-engine plane flying very low, in the direction of the White House. Sure enough, the plane flies at treetop-level and eventually smashes right into the Presidential home. Fortunately, the President and his family were sleeping across the street that night. Even though the FAA had information that the plane was heading for the White House, it went unreported. But wait up, there was a good reason—no one was watching the monitor when the blip came on the screen. The plane only showed up hours later, when someone thought to review the recorded log. If the President had been in his own bed that night it would have been the coffee break heard round the world.

○○○

Here are a couple more examples you can probably relate to with your own team:

Doug and Diane hate each other's guts. They have been working side by side on a customer service crew for a Chicago retailer for over a year, and everything they do gets on the other's nerves. Their relationship has gotten so toxic that it frequently boils over and compromises the quality of customer interactions. This is the opposite of the Abilene Paradox, but just as common—it is a conspiracy to betray. Doug is not passing along queries that only Diane can resolve; Diane, Doug claims, has deliberately altered information that Doug then passed on to customers. The interpersonal war goes on, and caught in the crossfire is the most innocent and most important of parties—the customer.

○○○

A cross-functional team at a Navy supply depot on the East Coast is honestly confused. Some members feel it is most natural to report to the team leader. Others have a pre-existing relationship with the champion who founded the team. Both "bosses" are on-site around the clock, and neither minds being reported to. Vital reporting issues are being blurred, and important information is getting lost, without a scrap of malice on anyone's part. These questions need to be answered: Who is the functional boss? Who gets information? What is the basis for sharing—the leader's need to know or the curious champion's desire to know? Who's in charge? This war of well-intentioned loyalties may tear the team apart.

Clearly, what is needed—besides the bare minimum good intentions—is an easy method for communicating better.

Learning to listen

When we think of communicating, we tend to picture ourselves talking. If only we said what we have to say more clearly, or more slowly, or simply louder—well, the world would understand better and we would get our way more often.

Of course, that is not what communication is at all about, at all. Good communication is a series of checks we run, first on ourselves, and then on the other person. Listening is three-quarters of high quality communication. When communication is really good, these four elements should be at work:[2]

Talking	Listening to ourselves listening
Listening to ourselves talking	Listening

✔ *Talking.* In our rush to be heard and understood, we focus too much on ourselves doing the talking. We are the critical factor in communication, it is true—but our listening is much more important than our talking, because it is our listening (whether it is good or awful) that determines the quality of communication.

✔ *Listening.* Instead of beginning in the familiar upper-left corner, with us talking, begin in the opposite corner, with us simply listening to the other party. This should be the easiest part, but it gives many people conniption fits. *You simply listen.* There ain't no better way to say it.

If you are having troubles with listening, listen up. The other squares, with the more mysterious labels, may hold the key.

✔ *Listening to ourselves talking.* Are we going on too long? Are we embellishing? Are we getting in little, subtle jabs at people? Are we "winking" in our speech, assuming things for the group that they

---

[2] The "listening" paradigm in this section belongs to educator Sue Miller Hurst, who shared her theory with us in a telephone interview relative to her upcoming presentation at The Masters Forum, Minneapolis.

perhaps should not assume? There are many sources of contamination in ordinary speech, and some of the worst crop up in team dialogue, where we are unconsciously working to express:

- our importance
- our superior knowledge
- our political convictions
- our prejudices, which we hope others share
- our disdain for the thoughts of a perceived adversary
- our insecurity about what others think of us
- our lack of stature in the group
- our unfamiliarity with the topic at hand
- our worry that someone is waiting to shoot us down

It is as if we have erected a wall around ourselves to prevent us from expressing our most sincere convictions. An encounter group industry exists to help people breach their walls. If you feel that you are consistently undermining your own best efforts, you might consider getting help of this type. There are a billion good books on how to do this, too. You can descend the interior staircase of your soul and get to work dusting the place.

For our purposes, however, we will simply remind you that whatever you have to say needs only to pass the simple test of teamwork: Are you saying something that is germane to the team as a whole—to its objectives, to its overriding vision, to the tasks it has set out for itself? If so, you are on solid ground, even if you are neurotic and still crave approval.

If not, fix your message so that it is *direct, relevant,* and *respectful* of others. People will understand. And lo and behold, the respect you have been craving will start to trickle in.

✔ *Listening to ourselves listening.* We are talking about developing in yourself a deeper skill of listening. This is a series of checks you run, as you are doing your best to hear what the other person is saying:

Are you thinking too much? If you are busy framing a reply while your teammate is expressing him or herself, you aren't being fair. Forget your reply. Do your teammates the justice of paying attention to their thoughts.

Are you leaping to conclusions? If you are insecure or hasty, you may be mentally finishing off your teammates' thoughts for them. This is rude and arrogant. Let them finish, and listen the whole time.

Don't analyze. You may think you're doing the team a favor subjecting its thoughts to your rigorous instant analysis. Quit with the analyzing, already. Think of a conversation as a garden, not a shooting gallery. You can analyze later, when you're all in the mood.

Don't be so cock-sure. We have a tendency to run what we are hearing against our internal database of what we know for sure: "That won't work . . . that violates Robbins' Second Law . . . man, is that stupid . . ." Who knows, maybe your internal database is wrong (just this once), and the speaker is right.

This fourth quadrant probably seemed fuzzy when you first saw it. We think it might be the most important of all. It is a check against your own agitation, your own ego-needs, your own impulsive reflexes—your worst communication dysfunctions.

Feedback

A subset of good communication is feedback. People, especially teams, need to be told what's what. Former New York City Mayor Ed Koch used to go around asking everyone, "How'm I doing?" It was his signature remark. He knew it was obnoxious—begging for affirmation gets old quick. But he was a shrewd fellow. He knew:

- the political value of being known for a single funny catch phrase
- the undeniable human appeal of being interested in the opinions of others
- the performance value of getting useful feedback

We're going to be looking at feedback primarily with the last reason in mind. But do not underestimate the power of the other two reasons. Feedback—communication, mutual evaluation, keeping score—is powerful stuff. Good, continuous feedback is like gasoline to a team ready to roll. The shrewd team leader keeps it pumping, for all the right reasons.

What feedback does

We live and work increasingly in an information-driven society. We measure everything, and we look at key measurements (monthly unemployment figures, Consumer Price Index, our kids' report cards, our spouse's Visa card statements) to see how we're doing, and where we stand.

Teams, too, need to know how they're doing. It is a kind of hunger, a voracious appetite to measure what they are doing every which way:

- feedback from one another
- feedback from team leaders
- feedback from customers
- feedback from the organization they are part of
- feedback in the form of numbers
- feedback in the form of words
- feedback that is scheduled, formal, and official
- feedback that just happens
- feedback of the long-term, big picture
- feedback on the here-and-now, itty-bitty picture

Feedback should be continuous, so that every team member has a living thread of information about "How'm I doin'?" that he or she can use to tailor a workstyle that contributes to top team effectiveness.

Good and bad feedback

Surprises. If you give a team member good, honest feedback and he or she is taken aback, something is wrong. Chances are the team waited too long before clueing in the errant team member. That's why continuous feedback beats periodic evaluations—mistakes don't have time to become habits. If you put off corrective feedback too long, the person in question will resent you for it. "Why didn't somebody tell me?" Semi-annual evaluations are for the birds. By the time people find out where they are coming up short, it's too late. And it feels just like Judgment at Nuremburg.

Soft-pedaling. The most important feedback we can give is often negative. But it's unpleasant. We daresay it is even more unpleasant to give negative criticism than it is to receive it—and that's saying something. The worst, worst, worst thing you can do is ignore it or minimize it. For want of a nail, the war was lost, as Poor Richard was wont to say. Replace the nail now, before a small problem grows into something humongous.

Good news/bad news. No one takes criticism well, so we have to give it with great care. This means walking a line between compliments that don't ring true and honest, helpful support. People can tell when you are "dressing up a dressing-down." When you have something good to say, focus on the good. When the news is not so good, be direct about that, too. It's pleasant if you can convincingly shore up an errant team member a word or two of friendly support. But it is hard to be convincing about such things, and there is the danger of miscommunicating the correction. The best thing is to say what you need to say. In the end it is the most respectful way to handle the problem.

A concluding question

Up until now we have been discussing feedback as a top-down phenomenon. Team leaders monitor their teams and provide regular feedback and evaluation. Bosses and supervisors from outside the team provide it.

Here's the question: *Can a self-directed team self-monitor?*

Good question. Without all team members having the designated role of feedback-giving, feedback becomes an ad hoc, undocumented, informal process. Not bad, but not great. Somehow a team must find a way to flush communication into their system. Chances are that there is a lot of vague feedback already occurring, and that it is useful:

"By the way, Georgia, I liked the drawings you came up with in the report."

"Rewrite this for me, will you, Dave—you're so much better at that than me."

"Ravi, I'm having problems with the file format you're using. Can we agree on a different standard?"

Even informal groups can create formal structures. A free-floating team can institute official carping sessions, where they can air out problems they are having with one another. Make it friendly, so the gripes don't overwhelm other kinds of feedback. And make it problem-solving oriented, so people leave feeling positive.

A leaderless team can have a process by which every member has another member to serve as a sounding board, with the idea that they meet once every week or so, over lunch, and discuss problems, worries, and performance questions. The two take turns mentoring one another. There should be a compact that the dyad be more than a back-patting session—maybe the team can draw up a series of hard questions to go over each time, so that the pairing accomplishes something.

chapter 14

•

rewards and recognition

•

saying one thing and doing another

The happy team books seem at times to be suggesting that it's such a great thing to be on a team that people will do it for free. Our observations do not bear this out. Work is an investment people make. They demand a return on that investment. If you do not pay them, they will not work.

No, pay/don't-pay is not the issue. The issues are *how* and *whom* you pay. Teams are a new thing, but except for a few departures (paying in stock, profit-sharing, gainsharing), not a lot of Newton-level thinking has been applied to compensation, rewards, and recognition for teams.

We shall attempt to apply some now.

This book's sole sports analogy

Consider the following fictional scenario, from Miami's Joe Robbie Stadium. This episode never actually occurred—we're just using famous sports stars' names for their celebrity cachet.[1]

---

[1] This example, and the principle of team safety, belong to Barry Leskin, vice president of Aetna Education at Aetna Insurance. We caught him at a session of The Masters Forum in August, 1993, in Minneapolis.

In this hypothetical example, quarterback Dan Marino has a bonus in his contract. It says that if he plays 50 quarters through the regular 16-game season, he earns a $375,000 bonus. Seemed like a good idea when the bonus was drawn up—the team wanted to reward him for staying healthy.

But here it is, the last game of the year. His team, the Dolphins, are tied for first place with division rival Buffalo. Marino is playing. The score is tied 14-14, but he's thrown four interceptions. His defense has been on the field all day. One more turnover and they can kiss the season goodbye. Marino knows his arm is hanging by a scrap of tendon, but he's keeping mum. Coach Don Shula grabs him on the sidelines and tells him, "I'm taking you out." Marino replies, "Do that and I'll sue you."

Huh? The problem here is that the reward Dolphins management thought was so clever came back and bit them on the behind. At a moment when every player should have been focused on the team goal of winning the division, the fictional Marino was willing to sink the team to claim his $375,000. In his own mind he was only doing what was asked of him. And a system of rewards focusing on individual action was about to undo the entire team.

Something rotten in the state of rewards

Despite some talk about team rewards, most team members are paid today exactly as they were paid in the days before teams, on a strict individual basis. We are rewarding individuals when we should be rewarding teams or the workforce as a whole. Not that there cannot or should not be "stars." Once again the 80/20 rule comes into play—20 percent of team members accounting for 80 percent of team success. But a successful team is always chipping away at the 80/20 rule—it seeks to get the very best out of all its members.

In the typical Japanese corporation today, about a third of all compensation is based on company performance.

We ask unions to help increase productivity when they know that success means decreasing the workforce, laying people off—the exact opposite of their best interests. We establish bonuses to motivate people, but the bonuses don't motivate because they are automatic or guaranteed. We patronize team members by dangling carrots in front of them. My, isn't that an attractive carrot?

We set up policies and procedures to instruct team members to do the right things without being supervised every moment—but we fail to shape a culture within our organizations that lets teams and team members feel secure doing the right things.

> *Teams will not carry out business objectives*
> *if doing so puts them at risk.*

Teams don't fail because the people on them are stupid. Nor because they don't enshrine the virtues of customer satisfaction, quality, and the rest. Teams fail because the people on them know it's not safe to go after their own stated goals.

The importance of security

What does "secure" mean? It means that a company professing to be serious about quality must not punish team members who undertake initiatives on behalf of quality. It means that team members exhorted to use their minds must feel free, and even encouraged, to disagree with one another and with management as a whole.

It means that teams encouraged to increase productivity will not be "rewarded" for their success with layoff notices. We want teams to "take risks"—but if the company is in a downsizing free-fall, how much risk are they likely to take?

Managers often think they can influence behavior based on quarterly goals or semiannual financial targets. The opposite is true; it is day-to-day culture—the informal signals about what is valued and what is not—that drives behavior more than anything else. So how do we un-confuse our systems of rewards? By getting back to basics and creating a system of rewards that reflects reality.

The challenge for us is to find mechanisms that can help us to influence team performance that are consistent with the strategic direction and priorities of the organization as a whole. We have flexibility in altering our reward system that we aren't even aware of. To tap into this flexibility, we need to ask three questions:

☞ *What rewards do teams and team members value?* The issue every team leader faces is how to get the people reporting to you committed to your goals. There is no one-size-fits-all method for achieving this alignment. Industries differ widely from one another, and the kind of people who choose to work in one industry—a government service bureau, say—are usually different from the people who choose to work in a sales organization. There are different kinds of rewards at different companies, because they want to attract different kinds of people.

People also have different compensation needs at different stages in their career. The needs of a 25-year-old are very different from those of a 50-year-old in the same organization.

What motivates people? Most people will chime in and say, cash. But it isn't that simple. Cash alone can be a feeble bond if the working conditions are unhealthy or the work itself is unsavory. For skilled workers there must be something besides cash on the barrelhead— security, the feeling of being appreciated, being left alone, pleasant working conditions, time off to travel. For some people the best reward of all is work itself—the challenge of a tough job. For some it's the interaction with other skilled team members. For some it's the intellectual gratification of addressing and solving a knotty problem.

Cash considerations

Cash compensation is still very important to most people. Three financial options that have met with success are profit sharing, gainsharing, and employee ownership. The idea behind each is to reward teams when they perform well. Each method has the side virtue of giving team members a strong degree of ownership in the organization and a sense of true participation in the organization's overall strategy. Each also falls short of the stated goal of motivating people to commit to organizational objectives.

✔ **Gainsharing** is a system whereby money or resources that are saved by a team are returned, in some degree, to the team. Gainsharing is in use at many thousands of companies. It links people with organizational success.

Problem: The easiest gainsharing plan to set up is a companywide or locationwide system. It is harder to measure the success of most kinds of individual teams in dollars—design, research, quality improvement, and problem-solving teams being exceptions.

✔ **Profit sharing** is better known and more widespread than gainsharing, perhaps because the idea is simpler. Every year or quarter, a dividend is paid to employees based on cooperate or divisionwide performance. Usually, the money is tumbled in with the worker's retirement plan or 401(k) plan.

Problem: Profit sharing is individual-oriented and organization-wide. It doesn't address team performance. Also, deferred rewards like retirement money never quite feel like rewards.

✔ **Employee ownership.** These plans go by such names as stock option plans, stock purchase plans, and employee stock ownership plans.

Problem: Ownership is great, but some companies aren't worth owning, even with terrific workforces. And again, this approach doesn't do much for teams.

Reengineered rewards

As organizations continue to reengineer and overhaul themselves, cash takes on a new face as a team reward. Tomorrow's team members will likely find that the new workplace provides less, not more, opportunity for promotions. Companies getting rid of unnecessary management levels will not be anxious to promote you to one of those evacuated positions. Thus, team members may find themselves stuck for many years in fairly static positions—by title, anyway. You may spend twenty years with the job title customer service representative.

Sounds terrible, right? But these twenty years will not be at burger flipper wages. In the reengineered organization, companies will have to compensate good team members for their vertical limitations with nice juicy horizontal rewards.

Think about it. A team member with deep experience in meeting customer needs will be a very valuable person, able to command substantial salary and benefits. Downsizing is a drag, but survivors who deliver the goods to an organization's customers will be richly rewarded. "I'm a customer service representative. And I make $140,000 a year."

Team-defined rewards

Management gurus insist that teams should not define their own reward system—"That's putting the monkeys in charge of the chicken coop." But we think it's an approach worth considering anyway. Team members shouldn't set their pay levels, for instance; but they may make valuable contributions to defining benefit choices and design recognition programs.

You may be a distinguished mind-reader and picked the perfect reward last time. Next time, however, why don't you ask workers what *they* would like as an incentive or reward? You can't predict what will light a fire for them. Consider team-proposed rewards as a kind of compensation laboratory. Yes, there will be some bad ideas, but there will be some that you would not have thought of in a million years by yourself, and the best will carry over to other teams as well.

Thirteen low-cost or no-cost rewards

How to let workers know on a team basis that their efforts are appreciated? "Cash is always in good taste," is a well-worn adage. It's also an untrue adage—reward a deed done out of simple decency or honesty with a few bucks and watch the look on the good-deed-doer's face.

Most team leaders don't have a laundry basket of financial favors to hand out to deserving team members. But there are still lots of no-cost or low-cost ways to keep team members involved and in the mood to perform:

- **Establish a prize.** Establish a quarterly "most valuable team member" award that teams themselves vote on. Establish a "biggest improvement" and "best team spirit" award, too—it helps keeps individual performance stars from getting all the attention.

- **Get 'em involved.** People having impact on reaching goals appreciate being part of forming those goals. Bring your best people into the planning process and they will walk through fire for you.
- **Power to the people.** What better way to spur productivity than to give proven achievers authority to spend a few bucks to increase sales, please customers, or improve critical processes?
- **Not rich, but famous.** Establish a "Hall of Fame" in your unit or department—a gallery of pictures, trophies, and plaques, with an emphasis on winning teams as well as winning individuals.
- **Praise in print.** If you have access to internal publications— newsletters, magazines, tabloids—get word of your people's performance to the editors.
- **If they had a hammer.** Everyone's dying for a faster computer, car-phone, or fax line. See that your top producers have access to your best tools.
- **Meet the boss.** Getting a chance to hobnob with the Group VP or even CEO is a big deal and shows you care about your people's career tracks.
- **Share the spotlight.** A pat on the back means more when it's up in front of co-workers. But be careful your reward ceremonies don't divide workers into winners and losers or over-stress individual achievement.
- **Privy privvies.** Everyone likes occasional "perks"—admission to the executive wash room, dining room, or gym. A parking place close to the building entrance. A direct phone line, bypassing the switchboard.
- **Free lunch.** Many companies purchase annual tickets to sports events, concerts, and other events, and many take travel, entertainment, and other goods and services as trade-outs. Why not share them with the people who make your unit a success?
- **Stock options.** If your company isn't up to a companywide stock purchase plan, consider a smaller-scale plan as a reward that binds your winners even closer to the company's fortunes.
- **Lavish them with attention.** Years ago, the famous Hawthorne experiments showed that people show more interest in their work when management shows interest in them. Paint the office, move

things around, invite juggling clowns for lunch—anything to break the monotony and show that you care.

- **Show 'em you care.** A good team works like a family and is fueled by respect and even affection. Let performers know their contributions are appreciated by you, personally. Look them in the eye and tell them that. It beats dinner for two at the Pump & Munch, hands down.

☛ *Who decides who is rewarded?* The greater the likelihood that the person you report to controls rewards, the greater the likelihood that person will influence your behavior. At bureaucratic organizations, this logical rule of thumb doesn't apply—simply come to work and keep breathing and you get everything that's good. Reward systems cannot be automatic or remote—to be effective they must be managed from close range. Are rewards stipulated by the same entity that measures individual and team performance? They should be.

Should team leaders and team members be part of the individual evaluation process? It is a tough call. People on the team have the best knowledge of the value of one another's work. But team members must not be put in the position of politicking one another for promotions and raises. Best to have the evaluation occur outside the team, with some evaluative information supplied from within.

☛ *What behaviors are rewarded?* Are workers rewarded just for showing up every day? For individual performance? Group performance? Organizational performance? Only a company with a narrow array of functions should be using a single reward approach. It's natural to use incentives to compensate sales people. But if it's good to encourage people in sales, why leave out support functions? The entire bandwidth of a company's workforce must be looked at to find rewards that push people together toward organizational success.

Rewards must be for achievements that matter, not noncontributing, non-value-adding activities. People must feel their work is important. People who cannot make the crossing to be more accountable even with training must be winnowed out and replaced.

Most organizations spend an inordinate amount of time trying to use their merit budget appropriately. One of Wm. Edwards Deming's

Fourteen Points, however, is that merit raises must be abolished. Not only are they destructive of team spirit—each member's raise coming at the expense of every other members' raises—but they just don't work. Splitting 4 percent into X number of even shares at the end of the year is not an incentive—by definition, you incent *before* the fact, not after.

This is such a simple idea—aligning your team's reward and performance with its business objectives. All it takes is clear thinking, some careful study, and the honesty to see what your organization is really saying to its teams.

chapter 15

.

depleted trust

.

why should i trust you?

In the Leadership Failure chapter, we described the atmosphere around team leaders who have lost credibility with team members. A single act of betrayal, and an otherwise well-meaning leader is hung out like a stinking corpse—out of the loop, ineffective, unable to perform any of the tasks of team leadership.

What is true of team leaders is true of all team members. A fragile thread binds dissimilar people into a team—that thread is the willingness to keep listening to one another. It does not take much in the way to constitute betrayal—a false statement, a misunderstanding not cleared up, evidence of self-serving above team-serving—to snip that thread.

Our first book, *Turf Wars*,[1] spent 200 pages talking about the challenge of getting people to work together instead of against one another. We named the book *Turf Wars* because we thought it sounded sexy in a negative way—people are intrigued by negative images (*The Terminator*, "The Fall of the House of Usher," Smuckers Jams and

---

[1] Harvey Robbins, *Turf Wars: Moving from Confrontation to Collaboration* (Chicago: Scott Foresman & Co.), 1989.

Jellies), and the image of an ongoing civil war within organizations certainly met that requirement.

If we wanted a more positive title we could have used *Restoring Trust in Organizations*. Because organizational war, and the deep-seated resistance one team or group may have toward another—or even toward itself—are what happened when the fabric of reliability between people begins to unravel.

Distrust is really a very rational thing. It can be described as the psychological dynamic of *closure*.

> *When we lack information about someone or something,*
> *it is human nature for us to fill in the gap*
> *with negative information of our own making.*

When I don't know you or your intentions, and your behaviors don't seem quite right to me, I assume the worst. If I don't know that you are telling me the truth, then, in my mind, you probably aren't. This xenophobic reflex or suspiciousness is a survival mechanism created by human beings to maintain their sanity—and to prolong our existence in the face of what is unknown and frightening.

In a team situation, loss of trust means instant banishment to a realm outside the inner team circle where no one pays you any attention. Worse, when what we are told conflicts with what we see, our belief dies. In the movies and in life, there is nothing more profoundly insulting than calling someone a liar. Being called a liar negates your existence and negates any hope of a relationship. With the belief dies confidence, rapport, the team relationship.

Stephen Covey[2] describes trust as a kind of bank account. It's a good metaphor. In a new relationship, each side begins with an automatic amount deposited—let's say $100. That amount in your account will grow immeasurably if you behave in a consistently reliable and trustworthy way. Or you can fritter away your $100 with minor acts of dishonesty and betrayal—before you know it, your promises and explanations come back marked NSF.

---

[2] Stephen R. Covey, *7 Habits of Highly Effective People* (New York: Simon & Schuster), 1989.

Restoring trust once you allow the account to deplete itself is a tall order. Like the boy who cried wolf, you have no basis upon which to rebuild trust, and you will be penalized—it will seem unfair to you—for a long time, no matter how honest your intentions.

Several movies (*Clockwork Orange* comes quickly to mind) have been made showing how a reformed individual will continue to be disbelieved and even abused after he has "gone straight." A single act of trustworthiness does not outweigh a single act of untrustworthiness—not by a long shot. You can't undo the harm of betrayal with a single act of heroism or generosity that will make everything else you said or did go away.

Nine strategies for creating trust

The very best way to repair a broken bond of trust is to not let it be broken in the first place. If that is no longer an option, you have a long road ahead of you, winning people back to your confidence. The only way we know is to keep slogging. Tell the truth. Keep your promises. Be reliable. Rebuild your account using regular, small deposits. It may take years of faithful, timely payments.

When you can't be perfect on any of these scores—and who can?—acknowledge it. Explain it. Ask for forgiveness. And promise to work to keep it from ever happening again.

As a prerequisite for building trust, team leaders and team members must:

1. Have clear, consistent goals

We said way back in Chapter 5 "Misplaced Goals, Confused Objectives," that a clear, acknowledged sense of where the team is going is essential not only in giving a clear sense of direction, but as a foundation for trust: If you don't know where you're going, that's probably exactly where you'll end up.

If I don't know what we're supposed to be doing and where we're heading as a team, my tendency is to be guarded and defensive for my own self-interest and survival. I will find it difficult to buy in to the team purpose and commit to other team members when I feel left adrift and uncertain. As a result, my trust level will be low. Having goals that are both clearly stated and consistently supported helps me establish a foundation of trust that will strengthen over time as the team moves in a predictable direction toward agreed-upon outcomes.

Many teams are plagued by a series of everchanging priorities and direction that leave team members bewildered and disillusioned. Many team members will find this inconsistency intolerable—and will resort in their frustration to self-indulgent, team-indifferent behaviors.

When this happens, it is important to step up communication drastically, to reassert the purpose of the team. Think of communication and trust as being yoked together. They rise together, they fall together. The less the communication during times of change, the lower the trust and commitment level of team members.

2. Be open, fair, and willing to listen

For many centuries, the Chinese had stringent guidelines regarding who got into heaven and who didn't. First, the gates to heaven were only open to Chinese leaders and royalty (peasants spent eternity in rice paddies). Before leaders could enter, they had to obtain a "mandate to heaven"—sort of like a Get Out of Jail card. One of the key requirements for obtaining this mandate was to be open, fair, and willing to listen to their people. This explains why, even today, senior Communist geezers nearing death have a tendency to loosen the reins of tyranny a bit (a wee bit—they are only hedging their bets, after all).

The same principle applies today in terms of building a sense of trust:

> *The more open, fair, and willing to listen individuals are,*
> *the more they are likely to receive the trust of others*
> *(both on and off their team).*

"Fairness" must be built into the conversation; people need to hear the word "fair" come out of your mouth: "I'd like the outcome to be fair to everyone." Or "It's important to me that people feel the process is fair."

Show a genuine interest in what the other person is saying by learning and practicing active empathic listening skills. Set up ways of making yourself accessible to others—an open door policy. These are all ways of starting the trust building process.

The injunction to be open, fair, and willing to listen is obviously valid for team leaders, but it is equally legitimate for team members. On a team of true collaborators, there can be no outsiders, secret-keepers, or (apparent) conspirators. Being open means, in large part, letting go. The history of management is the chronicle of a few individuals exercising control over the rest. It does not take a Ph.D. in psychology to see that there is an inverse relationship between control and credibility. Those with the tightest grip on the information at their disposal are the least trusted—again, the mind filling in what it does not know with negative assumptions.

To have credibility, you must relax your grip of control over others.

3. Be decisive—and how

Nothing sucks the air out of a team faster than having outcomes that need to be achieved and no one making any decisions to draw nearer to those outcomes. Particularly the person or persons "supposed" to be making those decisions.

Are you a fan of frightening truisms? Try this on for size:

> *When it comes to building trust,*
> *even a bad decision is better than no decision.*

People just don't trust people who are indecisive (see "closure" below). Sometimes, trust dissolves not because decisions are being neglected, but because the team objects to the way the decision was made.

Let's say a team arrives at a decision point in a project. One team member expects consensus. Another expects the boss to decide. A third expects some sort of sub-committee recommendation. What is this team in? Deep weeds. Team members' expectations are thwarted. They become frustrated. Then angry. Motives come into question. Trust is last seen taking the expressway out of town.

This may seem overly cautious but it is not:

Before teams can make important decisions,
they must decide how to make those decisions.

4. Support all other team members

Loyalty is a linchpin of building team trust. The concept comes from family life. If you've come from a large family (say, three or more siblings), you know everything there is to know about sibling rivalry. You occasionally beat up on your brothers or sisters. You also, we are sure, protected these same siblings from others who wanted to beat them up. That (the latter, not the former) is what support is all about.

A team is a family.

Fights will occur, but you keep them inside the team. You don't broadcast your dirty laundry to others. You protect team members from becoming victims of non-team member abuse. Given the opportunity to agree with someone else about a team member's errant ways, you stick up for that member instead. (Think about it: how much would that person trust you if you badmouthed your fellow teammates behind their backs? Not very.)

5. Take responsibility for team actions

This is a hard one for some team members to get. If something goes wrong, you don't point fingers; you take personal responsibility for the actions of the team as a whole. This is true whether you are team leader or not.

We know of one organization whose teams had a crest which represented their lack of trust. It was arms crossed in front of their chest with fingers pointing in opposite directions.

Finger pointing destroys
the very fiber of teamwork.

Blaming convolutes the team process. Who will speak freely, offer ideas freely, and provide honest critiques knowing someone on the team is going to come down on them with a sledgehammer? It's much better from a trust standpoint for someone to see you as a "stand up and be counted" type of person, not blaming others on the team for failures. Not, "our team doesn't make mistakes," but "our mistakes are team mistakes, and we learn from them and move on."

6. Give credit to team members

Albert Einstein offered this choice piece of wisdom:

> *Nothing is ever yours*
> *until you give it away.*

Meaning, if it's acknowledgment you want, be generous with what you have done.

Maybe the germ of an idea was yours, but didn't it require the whole team to nurture, expand, and apply the idea to the task at hand? The prima donna who insists on mopping up all team applause is probably a very valuable member—but in his or her very talent lies the seed of team destruction.

Shine a light on others on your team. But shine it sincerely. If it's done in a superficial or artificial or unctuous way (think: Oscar thank-you speeches) you'll kill, not cultivate, trust. But if done with genuine recognition for teammate accomplishments, trust will grow.

Can you be sincere? Can you share? Most of us are pretty selfish and self-protecting, so giving credit to others does not come naturally. It's something to work on.

While you're working on it, be very clear on something: one of the worst things you can do is horn in on another team member's glory. There is nothing more aggravating than to have someone else (like the team leader) take credit for your (or another's) work. A team member who steals another team member's thunder—what can you say?

Smart guy, Einstein.

7. Be sensitive to the needs of team members

Work is hard, tiring, frustrating, often painful. So we appreciate it when teammates indicate that they understand the pressures, and sympathize. We're not talking about pity, or playing the tragic violin, or treating one another like children. We are talking about fellow feeling—giving one another the occasional human sign that we understand and appreciate.

> *The best way to build up a strong trust bank account*
> *is by showing awareness of and sensitivity to*
> *the needs of other team members.*

Showing fellow workers that you are genuinely concerned about their struggles—at work or home—allows them to feel comfortable with you and increases the likelihood of reciprocal understanding.

On a less intimate level, it means being sensitive to people's practical preferences. For example, there is a best way to communicate with every person: face to face, in writing, e-mail, voice-mail, with a lot of details or not, with recommendations or not, etc. Let the other person know you are trying to relate to them within their comfort zone, not yours. It takes flexibility and thought on your part—but with a handsome payoff in their willingness to hear and act on your thoughts.

8. Respect the opinions of others

Not everyone sees the world the same way; in fact, no one does. When five people witness an auto accident, police compile five different reports. Each opinion is based upon an individual viewpoint. That's why there are five billion people in the world, not one very big person.

Other team members may come up with ideas that you think are the craziest things you've ever heard uttered by another human being. That doesn't make them crazy or deserving of disrespect because their opinion differs from yours. The best teams are made up of people with the biggest diversity of perceptions who first learn to understand and value the opinions and views of others.

> *Trust without respect is like a*
> *sandwich without bread.*

If you don't or can't respect someone, especially on your team, you will never trust them. People do not come equipped with RESPECT buttons they can push and be flooded with respect for others. Indeed, we are stingy with respect—"I can't give it; they have to earn it."

If you feel swamped by your own stinginess, what can you do? First, acknowledge the fact, and concede that it is as least partially your problem. Everyone deserves a basic level of respect, after all; if your nature makes you contemptuous of even that basic level, you may be *all* of the problem. *Hint:* people who lack respect for others don't always have the abundance of self-esteem that they think they have.

To learn respect, return to the fundamentals of goals and roles. Focus on the task, not the personnel. Try to build a narrow basis for trust on what a person commits to and does—being a good soldier. Set aside past bad behaviors or personality quirks.

Gossip kills respect. Often you will get advance word from the grapevine to "watch out for Charlie." Charlie's reputation isn't Charlie. Form your opinions about him by working with him, not from the vague rumblings of the lunchroom.

9. Empower team members to act

Team members cannot be empowered to act; they must empower themselves. As a team member, however, you can help create an atmosphere where other team members feel free to take risks and take action toward the completion of tasks.

In an organization where people are afraid to take action or risks without first checking with some higher authority, they will resist any attempts to "empower" them. Where team members do feel comfortable initiating action and letting their boss know what's going on (so the boss doesn't wind up with a face full of egg), trust starts to grow.

> *Trust given results in trust,*
> *support, and loyalty in return.*

Perceptions and trust

A moment ago—in number 8, "Respect the opinions of others"—we talked about how different people can view the same situation in different ways and arrive at conflicting interpretations. Obviously, when people are seeing the same thing in different ways, they start to wonder about one another. "Is he crazy?" "She is really deluding herself!" "Do I dare share my opinions with people who can't see the nose in front of their own faces?"

Perceptual differences between team members are a major cause of trust breakdown. To reverse this breakdown, we must first understand that our perceptions of the world differ for good reasons. We all *select, organize,* and *interpret* information differently. Let's talk about each one in turn.

Perceptions are *selected.* We are all constantly surrounded and bombarded by activity. Lights, noise, talking, wind, and even our own thinking are sources of stimulation that we can perceive.

To make sense out of all this stuff, we become selective in our perceptions. We edit. We block out the buzzing lights, the air conditioner hum, the noisy conversations, and the child asking for our help—and concentrate on what we are reading. When the child finally does get our attention, we re-focus, block out the rest, swivel toward the child like Robocop and say, "Sorry, I didn't hear you."

We select the stimulation that we wish to perceive, based on our *expectations, needs,* and our *wants.* If our first impression of someone is negative ("She sure dresses like a slob"), we tend to pick out those actions that support those first impressions ("Get a load of that desk"). We expect certain things to be true and sure enough, we find them.

If we need more office space, we notice all the vacant space in the building—space we never noticed before. If we want a new boat, all of a sudden we become aware of all the boats for sale along the road on our way home from work.

> *The most powerful word in the English language is the word NOTICE.*
> *If you don't notice your environment,*
> *you can't interact effectively with it.*

Once we've selected information, we *organize* it via two very interesting methods. One is called *figure-ground.* That is, one set of information becomes the figure we focus on and everything else becomes the ignored background. Figure-ground occurs when two people think they're talking about the same thing, but actually are talking about two different things.

Maybe it's happened to you. You're in a conversation with someone; the conversaton ends; you think you have an agreement; then fifteen minutes later, you stop, slap youself on the forehead and ask yourself, "Were we even talking about the same thing?"

Perhaps you noticed the other person doing something totally different from what you thought you had agreed to. In reality, you both heard different things from the same conversation based upon each person's pre-determined focus or priority. Each was listening to his "inner ear" rather than what the other person was saying. The conversation founders on the shoals of each side's self-fascination. The conversation is nothing but a "dual-monologue." It cannot progress to true communication.

> *What's important to us may not be*
> *what's important to someone else.*

That's where many misunderstandings begin. To stop this sort of misunderstanding, never end a conversation without first clarifying *who* is responsible for *what* by *when*, and *how* are you going to check with each other to make sure you're on track.

The second way we organize information is through *closure*. Closure is based on the principle that where there's smoke, there's fire. If we have incomplete information about something, we tend to fill in the blanks using what we already do know. (Smoke, therefore fire.) The problem is, we have a natural tendency to fill in the blanks with *negatives*, not positives. So if we get left out of a meeting or off a memo we feel we should have received, we feel the sender intentionally tried to do us harm. Sound familiar? The higher the trust levels, the less likely negative closure will occur.

Many times we see only a part of what is going on but will organize it by filling in what is missing. The parts we fill in are as real to us as what we have actually observed. This is why rumors are so easy to start, so powerful once they have started, and so hard to put an end to.

The best way to overcome this tendency is to check out the facts or ask for the other person's intentions the next time you start feeling upset about what they are communicating to you.

> *When we assume negative intentions on others' part,*
> *we react by "getting even."*

The next step, after we have selected and organized information, is to *interpret* it. Our interpretations are affected by the *ambiguity* of the situation, our *attitude*, our *orientation*, and the *psychological* context of the situation.

✔ *Ambiguity.* A man dashes into an airport bar in an obvious hurry. Orders a drink, slams it down, throws a $5 bill on the bar, and runs out. The bartender slowly walks up to the bar, picks up the money, turns to another patron and says, "Isn't that interesting. He was in such a hurry, he forgot to pay for his drink . . . but he left me a $5 tip."

Ambiguity: If you don't tell another person how you want them to interpret your information, they're free to interpret it based on whatever happens to be rumbling around in their brain at the time.

✔ *Attitude.* If you're like most normal people, your mood changes during the day based upon your interactions with other people or information. You may know what your attitude is at the time, but others don't. In order to enhance your communication with others, since they are interpreting your messages based upon both your verbal and non-verbal behaviors, you need to let them know what your attitude is at the time of your conversation. Some people have taken a 4" x 4" piece of cardboard and drawn a "mister happy" face on one side, a "mister yuk" face on the other, and hung it outside their work space. As their mood changes during the day, they flip the card back and forth. This helps those coming in to talk to better interpret their information based upon the mood of the person.

> *How things look on the outside of us depends*
> *a lot on how things are on the inside of us.*

✔ *Orientation.* We all have orientations or comfort zones in which we operate. These orientations may be made up of our experiences from where we grew up (example: All New Yorkers think and act alike, but differently than Midwesterners), our religious/ philosophical backgrounds (Jewish, Catholic, Lutheran, Humanist, Moslem, Atheist, etc.), our education (M.B.A.'s, Ph.D.'s, engineers, writers, salespeople, etc.), our cultural heritage (Italian-American, African-American, Latin-American, Native American, etc.), our color charts (black, white, brown, red, yellow, green, puce, etc.), sexual preferences (heterosexual, homosexual, both, neither, etc.). Our orientation is unique and makes us who we are. It also requires us to be sensitive to the orientations of others if we are to communicate more effectively with them.

✔ *Psychological Context.* This is a natural human trap in which we often get caught. Basically, we all interpret information we hear based on the last piece of of information we happened to be thinking about. For example, if a salesperson is thinking she knows what a customer needs (blue coat), she may unthinkingly ring up the blue coat—even though the customer only bought a pair of red socks. The salesperson wrote the order based on what she was thinking, not what she actually heard.

In factories there is a storage space set aside at the end of the assembly line. It's called the redo line, because it's where everything that has to be redone is put. It has been estimated that 40 percent of the cost of redoing work, across all industries, is the result of mistakes incurred because of psychological context—people misperceiving, seeing false patterns, unthinkingly turning a screw to the left instead of the right. We slap ourselves on the forehead when we make these completely avoidable mistakes—then proceed to make them again.

The lesson here is that team members must be very vigilant about their own attitudes. Suspicions that would have saved us from treachery and defenestration in another era become our workaday enemy in the team era. We must learn to identify when our instincts about one another are serving us well and when they are doing us a disservice.

It's OK to trust your senses.
It's your brain you have to keep an eye on.

Trust depleted may never be regained. It is a tough business—two strikes and you're out. When trust is gone, it must be replaced by control—rules, regulation, structure, 3-ring notebooks. The team spends as much time policing itself as doing its job.

A world without trust is a world full of "lawyers." Lawyers are society's artists of control. When team members forsake group concerns for individual experiences they fracture the spirit of the group. The "team lawyer" creates language that is frightfully clear, and frighteningly uncreative. The irony is that control ultimately fails to control—for who can really understand the clarity of legalese? A team that comes up empty in the trust department will start to think like a lawyer—not what works, or what is best, or what meets the customer's needs, but what technically complies with what is asked of us.

chapter 16

·

change issues

·

who's rocking the boat?

We are passing through an official era of reinvention, reengineering, and transformation. And we hate it. We hate change because no matter which of three classic responses we make to it, it wins. If we *don't embrace change*, it overtakes us and hurts like hell. If we *do try to embrace it*, it still knocks us for a loop. If we try to *anticipate it* and be ready when it appears—well, it doesn't make much difference, we still wind up on our keesters. Change is pain, even when self-administered.

Change is to a team as the ocean is to a sponge—it is inside, outside, everywhere, the milieu in which everything happens. Teams in most companies are a part of the change. Because teams are geared toward flexibility, they should be better able to deal with the difficulties of change than conventional work groups.

But it's still a drag, and many, many teams have perished because they could not adapt to the changes engulfing them. This chapter looks at the ways change can batter a team and ways teams can batter back.

Understanding change

There's not much we could tell an acquaintance of ours, Steve. He and his team were hit hard by change, and it exacted a terrible toll.

Steve had to move his product design team from a remote location to headquarters (some 20 miles away) while the manufacturing group they supported remained. This move didn't make sense to most of the team. The fact that the decision came both as a surprise and with short notice caused some anxiety and tension. Steve's challenge was fourfold: to take the edge off his team's stress, to weave himself and the team into the new surroundings, to not lose touch with manufacturing, 20 miles away, and to maintain performance while all this was happening.

There were many decisions to make and many people to contact in order to get stuff done. It meant setting up in a very short time a functioning equivalent of work processes that took years to get right at the old location. Considerations included supplies, copying, mail, carpools, parking, communication strategies, policies, procedures, name badges, space allocation—and where did you say the bathrooms were?

It took Steve three months and several economy-size jars of Excedrin to overcome the team's initial resistance, make the dreaded move, and settle down to business. Three months of pushing and pulling with various headquarters staffers who pretended they had just arrived from Mars ("And you're who, you're here to do what?"). Three months of tension, confusion, fidgetiness, frustration, hard feelings.

How did productivity fare through this disaster? Superbly—not.

By the end of their ordeal, which they endured with fortitude and resilience, they were wrecks—demoralized, exhausted, and vulnerable. And of course there was no rest period for them, because change never lets up. One wave engulfs you, and its big sister is coming up behind.

Seven hard truths

If you are serious about helping your team and its members increase their tolerance for change, there are seven facts about people and change that you must understand. When undergoing change:

1. *People feel awkward, ill-at-ease, and self-conscious.* The people best adapted to change are those raised in an ever-changing environment, like army brats who move every three or so years,

or research scientists seeking change with every breath. For the rest of us, change is scary, painful, and unwanted.

2. *People will think first about what they must give up.* It's a defense mechanism; the worst-case scenario. Team members will first think about what they have to lose by being on a team rather than what they have to gain. The job of an effective team leader, then, becomes one of painting positive expectations of outcomes to overcome this natural defensive behavior.

3. *People will feel alone.* Most people will not share their feelings of change anxiety with other team members for fear of being seen as uncertain or uncommitted. As a result, little communication occurs at the very moment (during change) when good communication is most critical. During change, the tendency is to hunker down and stiffen the upper lip, all the while feeling isolated and alone. When it comes to change, feelings are facts. Now is the moment to have team members get their feelings out on the table and resolved.

4. *People can handle only so much change.* We've worked with several organizations during major change times—some more successful than others. One of the keys to successful change is timing. Companies that dole out change in small doses over longer periods of time, hoping to minimize negative impact, are surprised at the sudden dip in morale after about the second or third dose. Even medicine given in small doses loses its impact in short order. Until team members can picture in their minds what their task and their role will be like when this change is complete, they will probably just nod their heads and not comply.

Organizations that have had the best success with change make major steps in short timeframes, with the end-product carefully described upfront. With this information under their belt, team members tolerate the short-term pain for the longer-term payoff. The "dribble" or incremental change method only heightens the sense of mistrust of management that many employees already have.

5. *People have different readiness levels for change.* Anytime a team is asked to change, some members will be excited and ready, and others will appear to have anchors tied around their enthusiasm. As we saw in Chapter 8 "The People Problem," people are very different from one another—how fast they can commit to change is just another way in which we differ. The challenge for teams is to boost the readiness of their least ready members, because these people determine the pace of the team as a whole. Any attempt to push faster will meet with increased resistance and slow the process. Following the steps laid out later in this chapter will help speed the change process along even for the less enthusiastic.

6. *People will fret that they don't have enough resources.* The first noise you hear from people in change pain is, "We could do it if we only had more resources." Sure, we all would like additional resources—but we usually have not made much use of the resources already at our disposal. Untapped, available, shared, borrowed, stolen, or heretofore unknown resources are usually all a team needs to get it through a tough change phase. Look around. Use the unused and underused. Make do. Or don't do. One nifty trick, after you've exhausted your search, is to go to the persons blocking the needed resources and ask for their input on alternative resources. Those who block usually know the way around the block, if anyone bothers to ask. They won't volunteer this information, but if asked, they'll usually tell.

7. *If you take the pressure off, people will revert to their old behaviors.* Momentum is an amazing and wonderful force. Like a compass, it keeps you going in the same direction. If the direction you're going, however, is the wrong one and needs changing, momentum can kill you. Momentum, like a magnet, will pull you back in the old direction, the old way of doing things. Change is a temporary force that pulls you in a new direction, but only if it's applied continuously until the new behaviors become the norm, the new north. If you take the pressure off

too early in a change process, the team will revert to the old way of doing business, old relationships, old behaviors, old processes, old habits.

Human speedbumps

Perhaps the most common factor in each of our lives is change. At work, at home, at play, daily transitions occur that make things different. Some variations are large and significant; most are small and simply intrude upon our daily routine. In order to understand our reaction to change, we first need to look at the *speedbumps* that slow us down as we approach any change. These fall into three types: *People, Processes,* and *Structures.*

Resistance to change is almost a fundamental fact of human nature. We wish this were not true. Resistance to the inevitable suggests there is something sort of stupid about us. But true it is. So the formula goes a little like this:

> *Unplanned change creates anxiety . . .*
> *Anxiety drags its feet in resistance . . .*
> *Irresistible force collides with immovable object . . .*
> *Team explodes in immense fireball.*

It happens every time. Well, not every time—few lottery winners decline to take possession of their winnings, to sidestep the changes that wealth brings. But most change stimulates resistance.

Most *resistance,* we believe, comes from at least a two-step process. First, human beings are creatures of habit, each one surrounded by an individual *comfort zone* of behaviors and interactions. Too much variation often means we must leave our comfort zone and face unknown consequences, which we have to evaluate. If we win the lottery, get a promotion, or find a new friend, most of us react positively. *It's where we perceive negative consequences to change, or continued uncertainty, that we resist.*

Resistance can come from a number of sources:

- **fear** . . . of failure; of loss (loss of identity, belonging, control, meaning, security, etc.); of the unknown; and of negative consequences such as criticism for mistakes.
- **laziness** . . . not wanting to put in the effort to make the change happen. These are the people who only see the short-term work required and become myopic to the *big picture* or the longer term.
- **previous momentum** . . . too much time and effort expended in the "old ways." This is the opposite of laziness. One is heading deliberately in a particular direction, has picked up speed, is feeling OK—then is asked to apply the brakes and turn in a brand new direction. This takes a toll on renewed team commitment, not to mention brake lining.
- **history** . . . dislike or distrust of the initiators of change. This is where "getting even" sometimes takes place. Either to settle an old score or just because you don't like the person in charge, you resist—actively or passively.
- **payoff** . . . no perceived return for your change investment (a/k/a *what's in it for me?*). Not only are humans creatures of habit, but we're a bit selfish too. If we do not see an advantage for ourselves in the change effort, we tend to wait the change out or not participate with enthusiasm. It becomes the task of *leaders* within the organization to clarify the payoff for each individual team member, as appropriate.

Process speedbumps

There are process speedbumps we keep an eye out for, so they don't bounce us off the road to effective change. These include poor planning and communication as well as poor follow-through and follow-up.

Planning and communication run hand in hand. You may have the best-thought-out plans around, but if no one knows about and buys into them, they're useless. Similarly, communication pipelines, either formal or informal, are just that—pipe. Whether they are used as sewers or rocket launchers is up to you.

Another potential process speedbump involves poor (or lack of) follow-through and follow-up. To become real a vision requires action. Just because you learned new skills in class, or talked about changing something at work, won't make change happen unless there is a *built-in* process for following through on action plans and checking progress (follow-up) at predetermined times down the road. This helps folks keep from falling back into their *old habits of behavior and performance.*

Structure speedbumps

Has anyone ever said to you, "You can't get there from here," or quoted policies, procedures, rules, or regulations as *reasons* why something can't be changed? If so, you experienced a structural speedbump. Most policies and procedures (Chapter 8) were created for specific reasons at a time in the past. Very rarely are they re-examined in the light of either current events or future goals and modified as necessary. Instead of being *cast in Jell-O* as was their intent, they're usually chiseled in stone. People come and people go, but stupid rules are forever. Modifying or moving around these speedbumps requires a careful mixture of Vaseline and dynamite.

Rules for Team Change

We hereby decree twelve key rules for reducing team resistance and clearing the way for effective team change:

1. Plan for change.

2. Involve others in the change process/get stakeholder agreement and commitment.

3. Communicate, communicate, communicate.

4. Generate expectations of outcomes.

5. Create influence/support networks.

6. Obtain adequate resources.

7. Generate critical mass to create and maintain impetus/momentum.

8. Follow-through and follow-up.

9. Persist and stand ready to pay the price for change—*mistakes.*

10. Reinforce early and often.

11. Keep processes and techniques simple.

12. Lead the way.

Let's look at each rule in turn and explain why it warrants the imperial mandate:

✔ *Plan for change.* We plan for change in order to have some measure of influence over it. We want to have a say in *where we're going* and *what are we going to become.* These are the questions team members must ask as they plan for change:

- What are our goals/objectives, strategies?
- How do they tie into the larger vision/mission?
- What resources do we anticipate needing—human, dollar, etc.?
- What is our implementation schedule?
- Who must/should be involved in formulating the change plan? How? When?
- What is the desired consequence of each change step?
- How will we know we've been successful? Can we give examples of desired outcomes?
- When will each change step be completed?
- What alternative strategies can we implement if "Plan A" fails?
- How will we deal with unanticipated events?
- Who needs to be influenced?
- Who will be involved in the change/implementation plan? How? When?
- Who might we use as blockers? How can we bring them on board?

As you can see, planning requires the gathering of a great deal of information from lots of people. The process of this data gathering has three effects on your immediate team: it involves them; it builds up an expectation for change; and it enhances their trust in the process because they can see it happening.

The problem is that once this planning process has begun, so has the ticking of the clocks inside the heads of team members who wait impatiently to see tangible change outcomes. Ticking raises stress—continuous communication becomes crucial at this point.

✔ *Get stakeholder agreement and commitment.* People don't usually resist *positive* change. We *like* winning the Publisher's Clearinghouse Sweepstakes. It's negative change—having to fend off a band of marauding baboons, or having to learn to speak Chinese in a plummeting elevator—that puts us off our feed.

To reduce resistance, try moving the change out of the shadows of negativity and into the light of day. Encourage team members to participate as partners in the change, and reward them when they do. Resistance will drop and willingness/commitment should increase. Participation can be active, directly involved in asking and answering the questions above. Or it can be passive, simply receiving continuous communication and feedback on the process. For example, bringing problems to the group and soliciting their inputs to possible solutions tends to overcome many negative expectations of change.

The most important aspect of involvement, however, is *getting people oriented toward the future*—helping them anticipate and embrace future outcomes. Determine all the stakeholders in any change and try to reach an agreement on "what *is* a desirable outcome?"

What will that outcome look, feel, taste, and smell like? Is it OK? The pathways of change toward the future have many twists, turns, and off-ramps. Encouraging people to help be the *drivers of the change vehicle* (determining what maps to use, what off-ramps to take) builds a commitment to the outcomes of change. It also allows them to move *within their comfort zones*—to keep the process moving forward. In other words, it makes the change their change.

✔ *Communicate, communicate, communicate.* Because human beings are such creatures of habit, taking them in a new direction or even improving their lot by providing them with "better" processes or enhanced information tends to make them a bit skittish.

Surprises especially build anxiety!

It's often not the *content of change* that people resist as much as the *process of providing it to them.* Even if the outcome of the change is eventually positive, people may resist if they do not feel communicated with from the beginning. Effective changework *demands* continuous communication—before, during, and after the change process. Anticipating and answering questions like:

- If this is our vision, how do we plan to get from here to there?
- What is involved in this change process?
- Who will be involved and how?
- When can we expect to see results?
- How can we be kept informed of progress?
- How does all this affect me personally?

Use multiple channels of communication to answer and update individuals so they feel less a victim of, and more an active participant in, the change process. Examples of multiple channels: internal newsletters, notes placed in pay envelopes, small and large open discussion meetings, ad hoc committees, informal networks and grapevines.

One technique is to place large hallway whiteboards where people can express their views and sentiments. This provides a forum for folks to express their concerns and issues, to clarify payoffs, and to provide inputs and alternative solutions and ideas. If it is not practical to involve all those affected, involve a representative sample—like a focus group—and provide a means to explain the *range and reason* for changes to everyone else.

✔ *Generate expectations of outcomes.* People have an interesting internal process that tries to match up what we *actually* see in our environment with what we *expect* to see. We pick out only those things that help us meet our expectations, and screen out the rest. If you can create a positive expectation for change or help folks see what any change will look like after it has taken place, they will feel safer and more secure when the change actually happens. They will also push harder to make sure that the change *does* take place and that it *looks like* what it was expected to look like.

✔ *Create influence/support networks.* Another element of successful changework is influence/support networks. You cannot create a successful change in a vacuum. Whether formal or informal, networks create both checkpoints and anxiety relievers for any change.

- Are we heading in the right direction?
- What modifications, if any, do we need to make in terms of people, processes, structures, resources, schedules, outcomes, commitment, etc.?
- Is anyone feeling a pinch about the change progress or direction to date?

Change usually causes one's comfort zone to shrink. But you can minimize shrinkage by expanding the support network and encouraging frequent use of it. Support can come from multiple sources (bosses, co-workers, mentors, subordinates, associates, cross-functional support teams, etc.). The more, the merrier.

Support networks have broader uses than just easing of personal anxiety. They can be used as *points of influence* to make change happen. This is where strategically placed *change advocates* can make a real difference. These change agents are people of influence—formal or informal—who *advocate for change* within your organization. Selling the need for and the rationale behind any change efforts to these people allows them to pave the way within their circle of influence.

Also, getting *opinion-makers* on your side makes it easier to sell any change to a larger group of people in a shorter period of time. Ultimately, these folks will help make or break any significant change effort anyway—so why not get them actively involved in the process early?

✔ *Obtain adequate resources.* Ask for help obtaining the amount of human and capital resources necessary to create and sustain any positive change. You may not get it, but you'll have tried. The research is very compelling on this point—many more actual requisitions are granted than nonrequisitions. Another benefit of asking and being turned down is that you may learn why the request was not granted—good information to have for the next request.

✔ *Generate critical mass necessary to create and maintain momentum.* Be aware of the number of people necessary to successfully carry off your change process. Two out of ten won't cut it. You need a broad base—unanimous within the team, and a healthy number of advocates, champions and friends on the outside. Once the change effort achieves momentum, use this movement as impetus for longer lasting or broader impact.

✔ *Follow-through and follow-up.* The best-laid plans of mice and men can go down the tube in a hurry if you are not on top of any change process. The process of follow-through and follow-up should be viewed not as a *policing* function but a coaching one.

Many people have habits or concerns that can get in the way of them making changes. This coaching process allows you and them to identify both personal and work-related barriers to change and talk about ways to address them. Follow-up can take place at either pre-determined times (once a week, month, quarter, etc.), or when people reach pre-determined stages in the change process (as when the phones are about to be installed).

✔ *Be ready to pay the price for change—mistakes.* Change means risk. Risk means mistakes. Fear of punishment for mistakes encourages "CYA" and reduces the willingness to take the risks necessary to make change work. Recently, a CEO of a major international manufacturing company made this point to us by relating a story within his organization. Several members of the engineering department came to him with an idea for a "better" process for making a certain component. It involved both new technology and a different process. It was a bit costly, but they were sure it would pay off in the long haul.

Having been delegated the responsibility and authority to make a decision, they did. It failed miserably. Several weeks later the CEO called these engineers into his office; they thought they were going to get punished for their failure. To their surprise, the CEO had balloons and cookies waiting for them. In astonishment, they asked for an explanation.

He responded that just because the outcome was less than expected, that did not mean their decision was wrong. The only failure would have been *not* to try new and different approaches, for, as he noted, innovation will be the hallmark of all their future success.

The failure was a short-term "hit" to the company but a long-term payoff in terms of unleashed creativity and willingness to change.

✔ *Reinforce early and often.* Being creatures of habit, it is impossible for us to completely abandon the "old ways" for the "new way" overnight. Change does move people and organizations toward desired outcomes—but slowly, in measurable steps.

The grease that keeps the change process going in a consistent direction is *positive reinforcement.* A word of acknowledgment, a formal recognition, a pat on the back all count as reinforcement—the ideal reinforcement is the one that motivates that individual employee for the progress he or she is making.

Reinforcement need not wait for completed outcomes. Ideally it is built into the process and awarded for *progress toward outcomes.* Public reinforcement of small changes, especially early on, creates the momentum necessary to reach the desired goals.

✔ *Keep the techniques simple.* The fashion is to say that complex problems require complex solutions. Maybe. But solutions that throw a team into an uproar, that take people too far out of their comfort zones, or are too technical, will result in great resistance. Like eating an elephant, complex change must be accomplished one bite at a time.

✔ *Lead the way.* Finally, the importance of leadership to successful changework can't be overemphasized. Effective leadership is a must for effective organizational change. We already mentioned the coaching function of leadership. There are several other requirements, two of which involve vision and pathway. Vision provides a dream of the future—what your organization will look like down the road.

Pathway provides some sense of how you expect to get from here to there as well as the impact on people, processes, and structures involved. Providing a way of determining the pathway to achieving your organization's future creates a lifeline for people to grasp in accomplishing changework.

The leadership keys to positive outcomes include attitude, analysis, and action. One of the sharpest arrows in your quiver for change is the attitude toward innovation and change that starts with leaders as they set the stage and attempt to energize others.

Creating an expectation for change as the *norm* for all employees (especially new hires) allows transition to be seen as part of the everyday process of conducting business. For example, some companies have created a norm of having a large percentage of their products produced from technologies that are not more than five years old. This stipulation creates an atmosphere for continuous innovation and change and guards against the bad habits encouraged by cash cow operations.

Next, ongoing analysis and feedback of progress toward outcomes keeps people fired up and on the right track. Finally, when leaders take personal responsibility to make small action steps happen, the entire organization becomes sharper.

Leveraging your change

The emphasis on change in this chapter may lull you into thinking that change itself is the goal of teams. It isn't. Change, whether for good or for ill, is the environment teams work within. Good change, or improvement in the goals, processes and output of the team, is the result of competent change management. There are several tools we can recommend for the effective leveraging of change:

✔ *Action forums.* As part of the increased communication required during periods of change, groups of individuals impacted by any specific change suggestion are gathered into *action forums*. These groups go through a discovery and bargaining process where they discuss the impact of the change on each individual, how to minimize any negative potential negative impact, what barriers need to be crossed and how, and how they can help make the change a reality.

✔ *Pilot projects*. The creation of a *trial balloon*—a tryout—is sometimes necessary to see what the impact of any change will be. Using small groups of enthusiastic people to discover real outcomes, before launching widespread change, provides a low-cost, reduced-risk snapshot of what will happen.

✔ *What-if scenarios*. The keys to successful change include *persistent analysis and action*. Your pilot project may be on the success road, but how are you going to monitor and adjust your change strategies as you encounter unplanned variables?

Lots of teams plan success scenarios. Few teams plan challenge scenarios. What if team resources are diminished? What if another company beats your company to market with the same kind of product your team is working on? What if team members are transferred, quit, or are unable to contribute? What if the market suddenly shifts, and the current plans become obsolete overnight?

This kind of thinking isn't much fun. Dwelling on negatives can erode a team's confidence. But most what-if scenarios are not catastrophic. Your team should have an answer in mind for various change scenarios. Using team imagination to think ahead is an important weapon in the team arsenal.

Dodge the potholes

The road to effective change is strewn with potholes, any one of which can throw your efforts out of alignment with your goals. In order for your organization and the people in it to have positive outcomes and build an "edge," it is important to *do change right*.

Consider following the 12 rules for change to achieve the commitment, momentum, and success your organization deserves. Your team's underbody will thank you.

part four

•

team

myths

chapter 17

•

the myth of adventure learning

•

belay that!

Rays of light spire over the humpback mountain peak, breaking up the blue sky. Christine stands facing the light, on the tip of a rock promontory, 70 feet over a pitted gorge leading down another 500 feet to a winding canyon stream. Falling means instant death.

As she greets the morning, the breeze blowing through her hair, she lifts her arms, teeters, and falls gently backward—into the arms of twelve groping team members, waiting just below.

Then the group trudges to the next adventure site, a pole Christine must climb in order to overcome her fears. Her twelve teammates will be belaying her with support ropes all the way. When the day is done, everyone who climbed will be awarded an ornamental carabiner, to put on the desk back at the office as a paperweight and a permanent reminder of the important lessons about teamwork learned up on the windswept slopes of Mount Cooperation.

Welcome to the heart-pounding, high-fiving world of adventure learning.

Adventure learning is a group event in which a team is put through a series of challenging physical and mental tasks. They often take place outdoors, in an idyllic setting, at a retreat in the mountains, or a dude ranch, or a park. They are facilitator-led, and they build on the psychological lessons learned years ago in '70s-ish, Carl Rogers' style encounter groups for normals.

Back then it was discovered that people could experience sensational breakthroughs in behavior if asked to do things they do not ordinarily do, with the rest of the group acting as support. The classic example is "Trust Falls." In this exercise you put a blindfolded person on a table, then let them fall backward, with the other group members catching the falling individual. In more complex manifestations, it can include rock climbing, pole climbing, rope bridges, and zipping down cables on a pulley.

There are two basic degrees of adventure learning, higher risk and lower risk; we'll call them "high ropes" and "low ropes." High ropes is the more adventurous of the two. It involves climbing mountains, crossing rope bridges, rapid descents on pulleys, and the like. There is some degree of actual physical danger in high ropes exercises—your teammates could decide not to belay you with their support ropes, and you could fall off the mountain.

Low ropes involves very little actual risk. It is adventure learning on a budget, usually a series of physical outdoors exercises that can be done in a park or backyard. They often begin with something like The Druid's Knot. Team members form a circle and then, taking turns, clasp right hands with the right hand of someone else in the circle. Then they do the same thing with their left hand. People are pulled very close with all the handshakes. The objective now is for everyone to untangle the knot, without letting go.

Usually the people most engaged in the solution are in the greatest pain, their bodies contorted like pretzels. Eventually they have all disentangled themselves and they form a large ring, much bigger than the original circle. From a knot to a ring; confusion to order—get it?

There sometimes comes a moment when the group simply can't figure out how to disengage without some people letting go. When this happens, those who let go become "blind." They must close their eyes and be guided from that point on by other team members—even into the next exercise! This is seen as a good teambuilding behavior—those with information assisting those without information.

(Some team "leaders" volunteer *others* as a sacrifice for the team good. "Igor, you let go now." An optimized team does not command team members to die for it; it does not even ask for volunteers.)

The next exercise may be The Spider's Web. This is done outside. A very long rope is strung between a tree, and then, through a series of loopbacks, is formed into a giant, semicircular spider's web. The strands of the web form perhaps 20 "windows," rather like the zones on a dartboard. The team challenge—to get every member of the team through the windows without disturbing the ropes. Two corollary rules make it even harder: no window can be used more than once, and some of the players will be "blind" from the previous exercise, and must be helped through, blindfolded. If you touch the web, you become blind.

Another low-ropes exercise example is called Acid River. The team must cross a raging imaginary river of acid. They have a dozen cinder blocks and three or four 4x4 planks. Using the planks, they can make bridges from block to block—but there are not enough planks to make a complete walkway to safety, so the planks have to be carefully moved back and forth as each person, small group, or team makes the treacherous crossing. Again, the exercise inherits however many people went "blind" from the previous exercise—and anyone stepping off the boards goes blind.

(We have seen games in which everyone is blind by the end. It is a very pathetic sight, grown men and women groping for a board that is right in front of them—the blind leading the blind, teammates to the corrosive end. It is pathetic and wonderful, by turns.)

These games are, first and foremost, a lot of fun to play. Most new teams are pretty stiff and formal with one another. They have never met outside the work situation. These games help break the ice and get people physically involved with one another. We are talking group grope here, and there are moments that will strike those whose noses are blue-hued as risqué, a sort of company-sanctioned Twister.

The lessons people learn in these groups include overcoming fear, overcoming distrust, and the synergistic power of a group working to support the individual. People who do this rave about it. They say it enabled them to do things they could never do. They say it changed their lives. Afterwards there is much hugging, exulting, people saying, "Why didn't we do this years ago?"

Everyone is ecstatic, certain that the lessons of teamwork will naturally translate to something wonderful once they get back to the office.

But . . . when the team folds up its ropes and packs away its carabiners and heads back to the city, *are* they a better team?

In our experience, they are not. People may be friendlier. They may feel that they got to know one another, out of the work setting. They may have lots of good warm fuzzies toward one another—which is good. They may head back with better intentions to team with one another—also good.

But they will not be a better team because the mountaineering or web-climbing exercises were not really about teaming. These activities were not developed to improve teamwork. They were developed to explore various dimensions of personal development. They are fantastic for achieving personal breakthroughs with one's own demons and fears. And yes, they are very good at improving one's personal attitudes about being in groups and allowing oneself to trust others.

But teams are not failing because people have fears and phobias or are unable, in a broad generic way, to "trust." Teams are failing because members are confused about what their roles are, what their mission is, whether or not they have the authority to do whatever needs to be done.

All this stuff with the carabiners and pulleys is great fun, and personally exhilarating, but pointless. Training firms that sell adventure learning for the personal exploration benefits are giving you your money's worth. Training firms that sell adventure learning for the teambuilding benefits are selling you a bill of goods.

You know the carabiner paperweights you get when you graduate from a high-ropes routine? We know someone with three of them on her credenza. Last time we saw her, she was heading up the mountain again, for a fourth. "It's such a powerful experience," she says.

So why does her team have to keep going back?

"Oh, we've got problems."

chapter 18

.

the myth of personality type

.

it's what's outside that counts!

We can encapsulate this chapter by saying that everything we just said about adventure learning and teambuilding also holds true for the Myers-Briggs Type Inventory.

Adventure learning used mountaineering and other outdoor experiences to provide team members with new understandings about themselves. The Myers-Briggs personality categories also provide every team member with exhilarating new insights into themselves, and a set of initials (e.g., ENTP, ISTJ) that explain what kind of person they are. The Myers-Briggs instrument is more than a piece of paper to enthusiasts—it becomes the organizing principle of their lives.

Typology is based on the insight that there are many "archetypes" of people, that those types can be tested and defined, and that knowing what type we are relates directly to such down-to-earth business problems as leadership development, career decisions, and just plain getting along with others.

Founded on the insights of pioneer psychoanalyst C. G. Jung, typology holds that people can be divided into two perceiving or input groups (sensors and intuitors) and two judging or processing/output groups (thinkers and feelers). It measures the state of your current nature/nurture stew. Knowing where one falls on the continuum between the extremes can help you in making career moves, in delegating tasks that are beyond you, in hiring and assigning people, and in working to strengthen your lesser talents.

Introvert/Extrovert	Thinking/Feeling
Sensing/Intuition	Perceiving/Judging

People are different, Jung says, in the different ways they encounter the world. Broadly speaking, we either intuit or sense as we perceive and learn about the world. Intuitive types grasp the truth of a situation in a flash. They are the mysterious beings who never took notes in class, who guess for success . . . futuristic and imaginative. Sensing types, conversely, grope toward understanding in a step-by-step concrete way . . . here and now.

In addition to these two perception categories, we are also either one of two deciding categories. Quick judges of a situation are called feelers—emotion is their strong suit. Slow judgers are called thinkers—their strong suits are logic and method.

Overlaying these personality traits are the categories of Introverts and Extroverts. Where you are on this continuum leads to assumptions about which of the characteristics above one is prone to reveal to others.

The kind of perception you naturally prefer, either sensing or intuition, tends to team up with the kind of judgment you naturally prefer, whether thinking or feeling. The total result is a set of sixteen separate personality types combining the strengths of the eight possible Myers-Briggs categories.

All of us, according to the theory, have two strong sides and two recessive sides. In fact, type psychology breaks us down into dozens of additional characteristic, with lots of hyphens and brackets, superior characteristics and phantom or inferior ones—striving desperately to make us stereotypes even in our complexity.

Why do we include Typology among our team myths? Because, just like adventure learning, typology has virtually nothing to do with teams. It is not that personalities are unimportant. In our chapter on

behavior differences, we stated that personalities are very different—
and when they clash on the job, in the team, it's bad news.

But the Myers-Briggs Type Inventory does not measure anything
that matters to teams. Teams do not rise or fall on how people are
(either real or perceived) deep down inside. They rise or fall on what
they actually do, how they actually behave toward one another on the
outside.

Behavior, *si*; typology, *no*.

The false assumptions the Myers-Briggs makes is that personality
reliably and consistently reveals itself in outside behaviors. It just ain't
so. There are too many confounding life experiences that modify what
we are into how we behave. Also, there is a large portion of our
population that delude themselves in terms of how they are viewed by
others. They say to themselves, "Oh, I'm an introvert!" Maybe they
drive through the neighborhood, shouting "I'm an introvert!" into a
bullhorn. But they're wrong (introverts don't do that).

All teams care about is what you do, in real terms, as seen through
the eyes of other teammates. What you are inside is your business.

A wise man once said it this way: If one person calls you a horse's
ass, well, it's just one person. If two people call you a horse's ass, well,
there may be a conspiracy to label you a horse's ass. But if three people
call you a horse's ass, you'd better invest in a saddle.

You can better determine what kind of a horse you are by getting
behavioral feedback from team members than by filling out the MBTI
questionnaire.

chapter 19

•

the myth that people like working together

•

heigh ho!

Say you have just been to a galvanizing seminar on teams or read one of the excellent happy team books that abound on business bookshelves. You are excited about the potential teams have. You decide to "go team" with your colleagues. You think, if we are to be a team, we must live, eat, breathe, and perform daily ablutions *as a team*. You tear down the cubicle walls, throw everyone in a pit together, sit back, and wait for those inevitable high-performance team results.

And wait. And wait.

You can wait till the cows come home, and high performance does not. The reason is that—surprise—people do not like being thrown into pits en masse.

We began this book with the wistful observation that most people have a real need, deep down, to work together. This is true in the aggregate. But we don't generally like being shackled to one another at the ankle. That's not a team, it's a chain gang.

People—average Americans, anyway—need their space to feel calm and safe. Spending the whole day in a playpen with teammates sounds less like a prescription for performance than a French drama of existential ennui.

Some of the most successful team environments we have visited don't feel all that "teamy" at first glance. In one highly successful team-oriented engineering company, the offices of team members are small, dimly lit, quiet, and include two desks facing away from one another. The engineers using the room are in constant contact, sharing information—but not smelling one another's breath. The overwhelming impression is of seclusion, not Team Monkey Island.

In designing a team environment, do not expect people to crave constant contact with one another. Honor their reluctance to lose their individual identity to the team. It's a fine line you have to walk. People must be able to access one another instantaneously. There must be no communications snags anywhere. But people need their privacy, too.

Be aware that environment matters. Find out what works. Chances are it will be about midway between the penthouse and the outhouse.

chapter 20

•

the myth that teamwork is more productive than individual work

•

the team! the team!

Teams are great. Cuisinarts are also great. But you wouldn't mow your lawn with one.

The great sin of the age of teaming is that people are so high on the idea of teaming that they are asking teams to do everything. A job done by a team is better than a job done by a single individual. You get that synergy going, you know, all that shared information . . . yeah. . . .

The truth is that teams are inherently inferior to individuals, in terms of efficiency. If a single person has sufficient information to complete a task, he or she will run rings around a team assigned the same task. There are no handoffs to other individuals. No misunderstandings or conflicting cultures. No personality conflicts, unless the individual is a multiple personality (see "Sybil Reengineering").

Beware. Teaming can be bad. Sometimes managers prefer teaming because it spreads accountability around, makes blaming more difficult. Sometimes it means a bigger travel and entertainment budget. Or it means hand-picking team members.

The saddest thing we hear is "We were told we had to do everything as a team." The CEO is all ga-ga about teams, so now unless you do something as a team you're a pariah in your organization. What's sad is that we hear it a lot. Mandatory teaming is misapplied team enthusiasm. It is anencephalic teaming. It is team tyranny, and people resent it.

chapter 21

•

the myth of "the more, the merrier" on teams

•

let's do the wave!

Some people think that the larger the team, the better the team. Wrong.

There is a trend in some companies to think of their entire organization as a team. This is an interesting expression, but not a useful one. Teams by their very nature can't be big. At some point they stop being teams and become mobs.

Team size is important. Smaller is much better than large. A team can be self-led, leader-led, formal or ad-hoc, but it can't be humongous.

A strategic business unit is usually not a team. SBUs can range from a score of people to several hundred, and they will be cross-functional as all get-out, and they will talk about themselves as a team—"We've got the Eastman Kodak Unit A Injection Molding and Extrusion Team Spirit!" What they are is a self-contained network of teams.

Harvey was once called in to talk to an SBU. When he entered the room, he saw 74 people sitting in chairs, about eight rows deep. Harvey exhaled.

"OK," he said, "who here is on the team?" All 74 hands went up.

"Uh huh. If something goes wrong, how many people here get into trouble?" This time only about seven hands went up.

"OK. You people are the team. The rest of you are adjuncts. Go home."

For his part, Mike was ghosting a book about the Malcolm Baldrige National Quality Award and had the opportunity to tour IBM Rochester, which had been touted as winning a giant proportion of points in its Baldrige scoring for its team orientation. The plant head had been quoted as saying that there were over 10,000 teams at the modest facility out on the Minnesota prairie.

So Mike drove to Rochester figuring he would walk down a lot of halls with rooms full of meeting teams. A city of teams. But after three hours of snooping around, he didn't see a single "team." The IBM Rochester definition of team was about as rigid as an amoeba. Whenever two people put their heads together on an ongoing basis, for a week or for a year, officially or unofficially, lean, mean, and transitory, that's a team.

Teams may sometimes seem larger than they are because of the adjuncts and resource personnel. These include:

- core members—the actual team, each one 100 percent dedicated to the team task
- resource team member—like the darting seagull, it drops its load and departs
- support people—people that help the core team get stuff done
- team sponsor—a manager the team can run to when it needs protection or direction
- team champion—this person created the team
- facilitators—outside people who help keep the team on track

This is not to say that an SBU or a department or division or even an entire division can't cultivate "team spirit." Heck, even a multinational corporation can call itself that if it wants to. It's a pleasant conceit, that sprawling, galactic, General Motors is simply "Team GM."

But . . .

part five

·

turning

teams

around

chapter 22

•

moving teams through stages toward success

•

the teaming goes round and round

Way back in the 1970s, psychologist B. W. Tuckman identified four stages of team development that he felt all teams had to pass through in order to be successful. They are:

- **Forming:** When a group is just learning to deal with one another; time in which minimal work gets accomplished.
- **Storming:** A time of stressful negotiation of the terms under which the team will work together; a trial by fire.
- **Norming:** A time in which roles are accepted, team feeling develops, and information is freely shared.
- **Performing:** When optimal levels are finally realized—in productivity, quality, decision-making, allocation of resources, and interpersonal interdependence.

With or without tests or team-building sessions, all successful teams go through all four of these stages. Sometimes a team gets lucky, and its mix of personalities, or the kinds of leadership that emerges among its members, brings the group from Forming to Performing with a minimum of struggle. But no team goes directly from Forming to Performing. Struggle and adaptation are critical, difficult, but very necessary parts of team development.

Identifying where your team is along the pathway toward success and how to move it from one stage to the next with minimum resistance are important factors distinguishing great teams from dysfunctional ones.

The forming stage

Forming is that stage in the development team when everything is up for grabs, when a team is only a team in the loosest sense of the word. The talent may all be right there in front of you—good engineers, good planners, good production people, good finance staff. But like a drill sergeant surveying his newest platoon on the first day of boot camp, you've never seen such a ragtag bunch of unsoldierly individuals in all your born days.

Did you ever, as a kid, transfer to a new school? Remember what that first day felt like? Walking to school you had one burning desire for the year, to do well, like Mom and Dad said. Once you took your place among all the other faces, however, all that changed. What mattered, instead, was being accepted by all these strangers. They were going to be important adjuncts in your life for the foreseeable future, and you wanted them to like you.

That overwhelming need to fit in, meanwhile, was met with a certain native opposition to adapting. No one wants to run up the white flag, unconditionally surrendering his or her personal identity—we all want to remain ourselves even while we fit into the group. We want "more information" on what we've gotten ourselves into. We want to know who's in charge, and what they're likely to require of us.

It's exactly the same with teams. We ache to plunge in, but first we need to know how cold the water is. That is the ambivalent mindset we bring to joining new teams. One of the signs of a team at the Forming stage is an overweening politeness, a bending over backwards to be pleasant, not to offend, not to ruffle feathers. Everyone has his 15 seconds of self-introduction, then sits down, eyes darting nervously. This is understandable when you consider that manners are generally instituted to keep strangers from frightening one another—

the hand extended in friendship supposedly is an ancient way of demonstrating that one is bringing peaceful intentions to the relationship, not a blackjack.

This eagerness to appear nonthreatening is really a key to how threatening Forming usually is: people getting together for the first time with all sorts of questions about which members have power and whether they will share it, and with whom, doubts about one's own abilities and the abilities of others, and prejudices about the types of people one is likely to be paired off against.

Amid these unsettling feelings, people cast about anxiously for something—anything—to form temporary alliances. It can be something as simple as two people smoking the same brand of cigarettes, a preference for the same vein of humor, being about the same height, or having worked with competing businesses in the past. Anything that pairs or triads can be used to derive feelings of safety from the larger group. (Forming is the birthplace of the clique.)

During the Forming stage, potential teammates identify similarities and expectations of outcomes, agree on the team's purpose, and identify possible resources and skill sets. They get to know each other and begin to bond, evaluate trust levels and, as much as possible, communicate personal needs.

The challenge of Forming is the challenge of giving an inert group of people who don't know each other a collective kickstart. Here are some of the questions which a group in Forming, in order to get going with a minimum of pain, must answer:

- Why was I asked to participate on this team?
- Whose idea was the formation of this team?
- Why were we formed?
- Who are the other members, and what are their strengths?
- How am I going to find out what they're good at, and also let them know my capabilities and characteristics?
- How large should the team be in order to accomplish the team goal quickly?
- Should team membership be voluntary or mandatory?
- How and when are we going to bring needed resources onto the team and get rid of them when they're no longer needed?

People who are new to one another cast about desperately for subject matter. All too typically they alight on the organization itself and establish some signal with one another that it's OK to poke fun at the company. Within moments of being put together they can be hard at work fashioning a caricature of the company they work for—so like the drawings of Teacher that got them in trouble in the fourth grade, still a way to achieve an easy, preliminary consensus twenty and forty years later. Someone or something must pay the price, serve as the safety valve, for the tension in a group just getting together.

Forming is a time of great danger. First impressions are made, and then set in concrete. Aggressive personalities move quickly to establish dominance. Alliances are formed, and counter-alliances. Signals are flashed back and forth, mysterious even to the transmitters. While the mass of group members silently mouth the words, *Why Are We Here?*, a few individuals may try to provide answers.

Besides team size and configuration, other issues must be resolved early on. Who "owns" the team? Does management own you, or do you own yourselves? By ownership, we mean commitment. Typically a new group has a weak focus on its sense of purpose and therefore has a hard time feeling very proprietary about what it's doing. In Forming, ownership is virtually all management's. But before a team comes full circle, it will reverse those proportions and will feel a bond of commitment so strong it will have at least a few insecure people in top management scratching their heads. The team must eventually belong to the team, not to management. Nor may it belong to the groups each team member (of cross-functional teams) represents.

The biggest monkey wrench a team member can throw into a problem-solving session is the statement, "We'll take that back to the division and see what my people will say." Yes, that's how the rest of the world works. It "sounds" good; it sounds responsible and politic. It buys time. It spares members the pain of saying no today. But it's not how effective teams operate. Members of effective teams come to the table already empowered; they wouldn't be on the team if they didn't have the authority to make judgments for their groups on their own. If a team member insists on taking every decision back to "the membership," it's probably time to push the button on his EJECT seat.

A final consideration: Who is a member and who is not? We have seen teams struggle with the drag weight of members who would rather be vacuuming the Mohave Desert than participating on the team. In some cases, it was because they were intransigent jerks. In many, many cases, however, it was not their fault—they truly were too busy, or they truly were convinced that another approach was better than the one the team was moving toward. But they were afraid to "drop out" lest they experience dire repercussions in their chosen career fields.

Management must be very, very honest—with the team and with itself—and it must say, in the most unmistakable terms possible, "No one will be punished if they decline to participate on this team. No recriminations and no ramifications, no loyalty oaths, no blacklists, no demotions. You have our permission to leave."

This is still not perfect. Few team members will walk away cheerfully, naive enough to think no one noticed them beating their hasty retreat, and no one will remember or retaliate for their departure. The work world will probably inflict pain on persons who quit their teams. That's regrettable. But the team is better off without them.

One of the greatest dangers of all is that someone in the group, a quick study, will want to push forward too quickly, to vault over Storming and Norming, and to go directly into Performing. The quick study may feel there is no time to waste and much progress to be achieved by sprinting to the finish line. But there are no shortcuts to team development. For now, the most important job for this team is not to build a better rocket or debug a beta version of a new software product or double sales—it is to orient itself to itself.

The storming stage

It is estimated that three fifths of the length of any team project, from start to finish, is taken up with the first two stages, Forming and Storming. In German literature there is a style characterized as *sturm und drang*, "storm and stress," referring to an exaltation of individual sensibilities.

The same could be said to apply to Storming as the pathway to teambuilding. Rank with individual emotion, group conflict, and change, Storming is not for the squeamish. The best that can be said for it is, it is necessary, and it gets things out of the way. What a team fails to settle during Storming will surely return to haunt it at a later date—and probably to return the team, kicking and screaming, to the eye of its own Storm.

There has never been a team that was not first tested in the Storming phase. And Storming always comes as a surprise, no matter how well one prepares for it. The best one can hope for is that it not drag on forever, as a gruesome war of attrition that no faction can win. To prevent this from happening there are some guidelines that teams still in formation may follow: Leadership is of paramount importance. If you are the leader of a new team and you leave them all alone to sort out their conflicts, writing them a blank check to take as long as the sorting-out takes, shame on you.

Now is the time to be stepping in, explaining limits, offering suggestions, keeping a lid on the inevitable anarchy. You do not want Storming to outgrow the office, spill over into the lunchroom, run riot in the streets, and finally head down the street, torches ablaze, pitchforks poised, toward the Bastille. You're not ready for that yet.

During Forming the leader's role was essentially directive—he or she pointed out where people were headed until the group could configure its own bearings. During Storming the leader continues to direct traffic, but he or she takes on the additional role of the coach—the person who not only tells you what to do, but helps with suggestions on how to get there.

Coaching is critical because Storming is where the most important dimensions of a team are worked out—its goals, its roles, its relationships, identifying likely barriers, and the infrastructure support mechanisms necessary to sustain long-term team health. Together with its goals, which the team began establishing during Forming, clarifying and implementing these other four elements comprise the entire agenda of teaming.

The coach is there to help, not to interfere. It is a delicate tightrope-walking act that he or she has to put on, because morale may dip to new lows and hostilities will emerge and demand some kind of reaction. One rule we try to impress is that you can say just about anything, but that personal destructiveness will be frowned upon, and probably squashed like a bug. Sniping, blaming, and belittling remarks that have no bearing on the work of the team are pure poison not only to the targeted individual but also to the sense of trust necessary for the team to function as a whole.

When you first see signs of personal poison bubbling to the surface, that's when it's time to call time out. People have work to do—tormenting one another is not merely wrong, it's irrelevant to the team's mission.

As with Forming, there are questions during Storming that need answering for the group to make progress. They include:

- What are we supposed to accomplish as a team?
- What are each of our roles and responsibilities as they relate to accomplishing the goal?
- Who do each of us need to get information from, and to whom does our information have to go in order to complete our goal? Where are our linkages to the outside world?
- If we get into trouble, who can we get to rescue us? Who will accept the responsibility of sponsoring this group and its activities?
- Who's in charge? Will that change from day to day, from one phase of the project to the next? How do we adapt to changing leadership?
- How will we arrive at decisions? When will we know we have done that?
- What happens when we fight? How do we resolve disagreements over goals or procedures?
- How do we increase our ability to take risks till we get to the most direct, most creative level?
- What strengths do each of us bring to bear on accomplishing our goal? How can we focus our strengths to influence activities outside our own team?
- When will we meet, and how (large groups, small groups, one-on-one, etc.)?

- How are we going to make ourselves more accessible to one another in order to complete our goals in a timely manner?
- Where (or who) are the team's supports? Where (or who) are our detractors and stumbling blocks?

A team that manages to answer those questions in the early stages of Storming will minimize the pain of a necessarily painful process. Remember that Storming takes as much time as there are issues in need of resolution. It is not a difficult task for teams made up of like-minded individuals—all design engineers, say. Cross-functional teams are by nature made up of primarily unlike-minded individuals.

Leaders might want to run periodic checks on their own status. Are they still the leader, or has a coup already occurred, without bloodshed? Often leaders are deposed, usually without animosity. If you are deposed on the grounds that someone else within the team is a more natural internal leader, chill. Chances are management knew this would happen all along, that your job, which was to get the group cranked up, has been accomplished. You may continue as a conduit of information to higher management. You may find you truly have become unnecessary, a sixth finger, and you may wish to move on to new challenges, or just go fishing.

In any event, these things happen during Storming. The only wrong reaction in such a circumstance is to get all defensive. No insult was intended. The group you helped form has made its first decision.

Leaders should understand the signs of Storming. Storming is hope mingled with a large dose of fear. During Storming, every team member is wondering if he is respected by the others. Some members will be hostile or overzealous. Some will be intimidated. Pulses will race. Sleep will be lost. Jealousy and infighting, competition and polarization are the orders of the day. Alliances that seemed solid one day come crashing apart the next. Some individuals will rush too soon into the cauldron and offer to be boiled down into "team." Others will resist membership, the compromise of their individuality, their standoffishness, as if their lives depended on it.

The worst news of all for leaders is that Storming extracts a terrible toll from them personally. Among the many charming occurrences in mid-Storm is a rash of blaming that generally trashes leadership at all levels. Suddenly, you're the reason the group can't coalesce, you're the reason deadlines aren't met, you're the reason individuals feel unfulfilled, misunderstood, deadended. As team members wrestle with their identity and direction, leaders are led out for judgment, sometimes gagged and bound.

We have seen leaders go white-knuckled with rage at the accusations teams trumped up as part of their rite of passage. You weren't there when we needed you is a common refrain. You only cared about yourself, they say, to an individual who may have lost sleep every night for a year because they couldn't get their act together, while the leader grappled with deciding how to intervene, and whether to intervene.

It can be hilarious to watch when a leader who has been patronizing his team is suddenly made aware of that fact (hilarious so long as you're not the leader, anyway). More often, though, it's just a painful ordeal. Like all developmental stages, there is no alternative to riding out the Storm. If it is any comfort, we offer to leaders the solace that what at first sight appeared to be a personality conflict is really nothing of the sort. And that may be the saving beauty of Storming—it truly is about team formation and only superficially about personalities.

One of the most challenging events in the life of a team is the introduction of new members. Say that your team got through the Storming phase—it took six months from your company's lifeblood. The very last thing you want to see happening with that project is a return to those halcyon days of yore. But that's what often happens when someone new is thrown in with an established team. That person will say things like, "But that isn't how we did it at Hyperion," and "We need to talk about some of these procedures from the ground up."

It's human nature to want new team members to feel welcome and for them to be quickly and cleanly folded in with the rest of the group. But their earnest suggestions that the game return to GO and start over again may have to be resisted, or redirected. The very best thing to do with new team members is to take them aside, for a week if necessary, and bring them up to speed on the history of the team, the decisions it has made and committed itself to, and the reasons why it is perilous to drag them all back to Square One in order to help orient a single new member.

Some people will object that it is too expensive to train new people so exhaustively, to answer all their questions, that "they won't be able to absorb" all the new information in one fell swoop. The answer is that it is far more expensive to leave the newcomer with a head full of questions, and the potential any loose cannon has to blow a hole through the deck.

Another option is what we call the "modified limited backslide," in which you permit the group to reenter the Storming phase in order to orient new individuals or rehash an unsolved problem, but with the strong proviso that Storming be brought to a clear conclusion by a pre-set deadline. You may have to swallow hard before you take this step, but sometimes, when the group shows signs it needs to reevaluate its direction, it is imperative. If you do not signal a retreat, the troops will bug out on their own.

Storming is the stage at which a few people will decide to stonewall. They still show up for work, and they may still communicate with other team members, after a fashion. But if you look closely at their behaviors, it becomes clear that the team at hand is not the team they wanted, so they have decided against being enthusiastic members.

Sometimes an entire team graduates from storming except for one individual, yet it finds itself unable to go on to the next stage—the holdout has them all by the shirt-tails, keeping them in place, while she storms on. For an individual like this, there are only two sensible options—to get with the team, or get out. At the same time, the team and the company owe her a second chance, maybe even a third chance, to reconsider her standoffishness and join the team.

Perhaps the worst consequence of Storming is that production may be at a standstill for weeks, even months at a time. For management, that is the bottom line of Storming—wasted time and blown projects. Somehow this chaotic process must be kept from mutating into ongoing turmoil.

To the extent that we can say that the process of teamwork works, it is in the minimizing of this necessary but painful period in the life of a group. The best analogy we have yet heard for Storming is that it is like internal combustion. If you place a teaspoon of gasoline on a sidewalk it quickly disperses, more or less harmlessly. Compressed in an engine cylinder, however, its vaporized particles begin to bounce into one another at supersonic speeds. Ideally, a controlled explosion occurs, and a vehicle many thousands of times the weight and size of that teaspoon of fuel begins to move.

When that happens, the Storm has broken. Roles clarify. A team style begins to materialize. The sun returns to the sky, and a calmer, new day dawns for everyone.

The norming stage

With the passing of the storm comes a new alignment and acceptance of roles within the team. The success experienced during the Norming stage is a success marked by contradiction—that the group becomes stronger as individuals let down key defenses, acknowledge weaknesses, and ask for help from people with compensating strengths.

The Norming stage is defined by acceptance of the very roles that Storming raged against. Relationships that began in the Forming stage as superficial events—coincidences of cigarette brands, favorite jokes, and alma maters—have the opportunity to deepen during Norming.

What's more, the group itself can finally be said to have a relationship with itself. It can show affection for individual members in the form of banter and repartee and genuine consideration. During Norming the ragged edges of conflict begin to subside. Tension ebbs, and many individuals now poke their heads out, like forest creatures after a summer downpour, to realize it is OK to come out of hiding.

What has happened is that the hidden agendas covertly advanced by members during Storming ("I want to lead," "I want to be left alone," "I reserve the right to disagree on any subject at any time") have been unmasked or have diminished in importance. People's needs to assert their dominion over the group, whether actively or passively, shrink in proportion to the growth of their intimate knowledge of the group.

As the group becomes less threatening, individual members mount fewer threats against it. Even individuals who are still conflicted tend to keep conflict from bubbling over and affecting other people's work—people take care not to derail or sabotage the hard-won feeling of teamhood the group now enjoys.

As group members become more docile, so does the group as a group gain in focus and unanimity. A splendid dynamic of peeling-away occurs, in which every dismantled individual defense is used to shore up the group instead. Weaknesses are reconstituted as strengths. Information is freely shared, and the group conducts periodic agenda checks to remind itself of its goals and take note of its progress.

During Forming leaders were critical to get the group going. During Storming leaders were the sacrificial victim, as struggling teams groped to achieve consensus at the leaders' expense. Now, during Norming, formal leadership begins to fade, as important data is no longer exclusive to leadership. In the next stage, Performing, leadership becomes a part of everyone's job, and mutual interdependence becomes the order of the day.

For the first time, the group may be pictured as a kind of great hulking beast, now able to move in a single direction, if haltingly, upon command. Before long, the great beast will be doing the marengue. For the first time, the group is a true team.

The performing stage

There is no guarantee that your team will make it as far as Performing. As Hamlet said, in one of his reveries on team-playing, "'Tis a consummation devoutly to be wished." The workforces of America are riddled with teams that never emerge from Storming, who continue to batter or ignore one another. They may call what they are doing every day from nine to five Performing, but the numbers are never there, and neither is the feeling.

Performing is not workaholism. In a way, it's the opposite, because it is the admission by every member of the team that he or she cannot do the job all by himself or herself. This is a level of genuine commitment to company goals and objectives that may be new to individual team members. A workaholic, by contrast, is someone who works every weekend. Workaholics think they're indispensable and the rest of the world are morons.

Performers know the real worth of everyone they work with. Performing team members don't get all bent out of shape if they're called over the weekend to help solve a pressing problem. Performing means being sufficiently in touch with one's own needs and requirements that one can fashion a work schedule that assures progress in team projects, without twisting one's own priorities beyond recognition.

Performing is a time of great personal growth among team members. With the sharing of the experiences, feelings, and ideas of other team members comes a new level of consciousness—the sense of knowing where other team members are at, a sense of fierce loyalty even to members you may not be friendly with, and a willingness to find a way through nearly any challenge that arises.

Performing means that the team becomes "fly-eyed"—seeing with many eyes instead of just two. This means a reduction in blind spots. It means that the team, encountering an elephant blindfolded, will be able to identify it as exactly what it is—an elephant.

Performing means intimacy. With performing, members may move beyond the locker-room banter of playful teasing into a dimension of communicating that is less self-conscious and less afraid. The humor may linger on, but the little missiles we fire at one another throughout the workday may be disarmed. The humor will reflect a lesser degree of veiled aggression and a greater degree of caring. Intimacy means understanding that a job is much more than "a job"—that one's pride, livelihood, and chances for happiness, security, and fulfillment are all riding on these balky contracts with our employers.

Intimacy means acknowledging the seriousness of individual team members' requirements, and pooling together to help ensure that every member succeeds, with the help of every other member. Conflict does not filter into the upper atmosphere during Performing. Indeed, it is more in evidence than ever. Perhaps it is because it is put on the table and not reshuffled into the deck that Performing works so well. Disagreements are confronted, discussed, considered, and adjudicated.

What during Storming seemed destructive—people at odds over project and turf issues—seems during Performance to be healthy and positive. Once the argument is resolved, team members resume working together. Losing an argument doesn't mean you get roasted; winning doesn't mean you get to scorch the loser. The order of the day during performing is "a good, clean fight." The atmosphere is one of enthusiasm and *esprit de corps*.

Best of all, apart from all this progress in the feel-good dimension is that the team is going great guns. Deadlines are being met, production is up to par, and the speed of information flow defies the usual mechanism of memo routing, weekly meetings, and quality checks. People are getting their work done properly, on time, and in coordinated sequence.

And the word goes out throughout the company, throughout the region: *Look out for the team over in* [your project name goes here]; *I think they're on to something.*

They're on to something, alright. It's called teamwork.

chapter 23

•

teams and technology

•

the 24-hour transworld team

In the old days—say, 20 years ago—team processes were slow but simple. People worked together, met together, spent Miller Time together—they virtually lived together. The team was probably all male, all white, and all of them—Bob, Tom, Al, and Dave—all drove to the same bedroom community when the working day was done.

Not no more. A handful of mighty forces have broken up the old gang. Some companies have gone global, spreading workteams across a score or more of time zones, and three or four continents. Telecommuting has undermined the sense of home-office solidarity. Corporate alliances with strategic partners mean that team members may not even be working for the same company. The move toward workplace diversity has further stirred the stew. A team today is about as mixed up as a team could be. And the most obvious victim of this mix-up is the Monday morning meeting. Bob is still on the team, but he is joined by Christine, Charlie, Abdul, and Xiaoping, a subteam in Sweden, and auxiliary members at a dozen partner organizations, three of them in Singapore.

They are scattered across the face of the globe. English is not the first language for the majority of team members. They come from different cultures, with different assumptions. They live in different time zones. They are paid in different money.

Go, team.

Technology is what made this kind of global teamwork possible, of course. With luck, technology just might help it all work.

The age of groupware

It's hard to come up with a technology phrase that means so much and connotes so little as the word groupware. Groupware is PC software for groups. To date, groupware products have addressed two main problems, controlling workflow (process) and regulating work content (substance), or some combination of the two.

Sometimes people designate ordinary LAN-network software like WordPerfect and Lotus 123 as groupware. Once they are loaded on a network, a team can access one another's files. But that doesn't make them groupware. To be a true group, people have to be a team, continually adding value to one another's efforts. A crew of clerical workers sharing a hard disk and a database or word processing program do not satisfy that team definition. LAN-ware is "shared-ware," not groupware.

There are four distinct types of groupware, described according to when each is used, and where. They are:

✔ *Same Time/Same Place.* The conventional meeting—team members sitting together in a room and talking—is the ultimate and the archetypal Same Time/Same Place technology.[1]

But in the new age adawning, the conventional meaning of meetings is giving way to different places and different times. And the factor that is allowing this to happen—indeed, forcing it to happen—is good old technology.

One of the most interesting true Same Time/Same Place applications is game show response systems, such as on *America's*

---

[1] We first encountered the time/place groupware continuum in a report by Groupware Users' Project, 1989. For vividness, clarity, and social strokes, nothing will ever take its place.

Funniest Home Videos, during which the studio audience, using voting keypads installed in their chairs, actually votes on which videos are the best.

Another Same Time/Same Place team tool is electronic meeting systems (EMS) that allow teams to think together, plan together, and decide together. At the high end are "Arizona Room" products—multimedia decision and planning laboratories used for brainstorming, issue analysis, prioritizing, policy formation, and stakeholder identification. A team of ten people, with ten connected PCs, can simultaneously co-create a document or action plan. It is a remarkable process to witness.

At the low end are laptop-borne meeting programs that help teams get their thoughts in order, prioritize them, and then vote on whatever action is to be taken.

✔ *Same Time/Different Place.* This is technology that allows people to communicate simultaneously across distance. It was the miracle of the ages once—the telegraph, the telephone, ham radio. Before that, we relied on smoke signals and drums. More recent developments: two-way video, screen sharing, teleconferencing. FAXes that you respond to immediately.

✔ *Different Time/Same Place.* Programs that team members can plug into on-site, at a time of their choosing. Any multiple-input, round-the-clock system. A Post-It note tabbed to the chair of the worker sitting at your desk during the shift after yours. The office itself, with all its books, tools, and support systems, is a technology meeting this definition.

One of the first electronic steps away from Same Time/Same Place team action was also one of the most significant—single-site networking, such as at a plant where three shifts of workers must somehow be in constant communication, around the clock. The solution, first implemented back in the 1960s, was the beginning of what we call e-mail. By using an internal, non-realtime communications system like Lotus' cc:Mail or Microsoft Mail, people within a large corporate complex no longer have to reserve a conference room to put their heads together.

✔ *Different Time/Different Place.* Networking, of course, quickly moved beyond a single site. In so doing it paved the way for the development of workgroup computing systems like Lotus Notes, a powerful messaging, planning, and organizing tool. Notes is the avatar of a whole new era of groupware products that will link networked teams together across time and space. But Notes, while flexible and easy to use, still represents the tip of the iceberg of the new meeting technologies.

Other examples: Voice Mail, Electronic Bulletin Board Systems (BBSs), online services like America Online, Prodigy, and Compuserve. Internet Gateways. FAXes that you respond to, but not immediately, like those dispatched in Europe the night before.

This is the most-publicized groupware grouping, but the technologies are still young. Once its potential is better understood, it will be a dominant force in the way teams use computers.

Does technology work?

Deciding what technology is best for your team is an immense question, involving everything that is on the market now, from software programs, hardware platforms, and phone/fax setups to pencils and erasers. We can't go through all that. But we can ask some diagnostic questions about the technology you currently have in place and whether it is helping the team be a team, or hindering it.

The PC network is the greatest empowerment force out there right now. Ideally, it allows people spread far apart to be sharing information 24 hours a day. It frees individuals from arduous rote tasks and allows them to use parts of the brain higher up the stem. Some perfect combination of phones, faxes, computers, modems, and group software products can lift your team to remarkable levels of achievement. But chances are, you've got the wrong combination in place.

✔ *Does your team run your computer system, or does the computer system run your team?* You want your people to be functioning like adults, not reduced to tears by some idiot batch command loop that they can't get out of. A great system is one which people can log onto, access what they need, and change what needs changing, without having to call in the system administrator. As your processes evolve, your system should be able to evolve with it. Problem is, most networks are still much too hard to use.

✔ *Is the team really more productive, or do they just look busy?* This is the biggie. Labor statistics say that office automation is leading the 1994 upsurge in productivity. Downsizing, the shucking off of unneeded personnel, and teaming, the elimination of the supervisory level, are offshoots of this surge. But not every activity belongs on-screen. Lots of activities still work better the old way—paper calendars, yellow legal pads, and No. 2 pencils.

✔ *Are security concerns undoing the benefits of your network?* Teams thrive on trust. Your LAN is supposed to put people in constant touch with one another, via e-mail, shared data, and computer conferencing. Too many levels of passwords, too obsessive an attitude about data security, can effectively lock people away from one another—putting your budding workteam right back on square one.

✔ *Are teams properly trained, or are they put out there to sink or swim?* Most team members need training, and not just on-the-job. Microsoft Excel, Lotus Notes, and the Internet are not intuitive ideas, no matter what your tech consultant told you. Bad training begets inefficiency and error. Some organizations have been successful by having workers who are already expert at key programs and technologies and take leadership in training the incoming.

✔ *Are team suggestions welcome, invited, rewarded?* It's to an organization's advantage to make team members lightning rods for process improvements, including technological processes. If team members come up with tips on how to use the software more efficiently, or how to move data from place to place with fewer problems, solicit them, and spread the word.

✔ *Is improved communications messing people up?* You can have too much of a good thing. Many teams have exulted in their new internal bulletin board system, or voicemail setup, only to be capsized by the torrent of messages. New Internet subscribers often complain about logging in to perform a task but first having to wade through 100 e-mail messages.

Technology can also undercut team feeling. Computers are a great help for teams scattered across a wide area, but they can put a real dent in teams occupying the same quarters. E-mail is great, but nothing beats good old face-to-face conversation. There is no such thing (yet) as a virtual water cooler or a digital bull session.

✔ *Has freedom led to chaos?* A team member turns telecommuter, and now works from home. To some extent he now manages himself, but not completely. How do you keep people you never break bread with connected and in touch with team goals? Has your company devised a plan to keep all its lone rangers from galloping off in a dozen different directions?

And how does a team leader practice MBWA—managing by walking around—when around is so far around?

What used to be a team of people working 9 to 5 in the same shoebox is now a bewildering array of all kinds of people working all sorts of crazy hours, reporting in a variety of different ways. Workers in such conditions require more attention, not less.

✔ *Is your PC system a substitute for real change?* The blessing of PCs is that they can cut employees loose from order-giving, double-checking, top-down hierarchies: "Do this and don't ask questions." But they work all right with old-style pre-team structures, too. "Computer sweatshop" is not a contradiction of terms. Don't assume, just because your team is hooked up to the latest network technology, that they know it's OK now to think. Let your computers be clones and your people be people.

Taking the technology plunge

There are several nagging questions about groupware. The biggest is, *Does our team need it?* Most teams know what their communications failings are and have a pretty good idea what role the tools of communication play in that failure. But unless they have read a rave review of Lotus Notes, or Microsoft Mail, or some new videoconferencing technology, what's available on the store shelf seems unnecessarily complicated, time-consuming, and difficult. Not to mention expensive.

Our observation is that team technologies are seldom requested by the team in question; they are usually imposed from the organization above. Few teams of eight or a dozen members can requisition a program like Notes, costing many thousands of dollars. But many companies decide that, henceforward, all teams will be linked via Notes (or MCI Mail, or some homegrown BBS system).

As we have suggested before, imposing solutions on teams undercuts the flexibility we want from teams. How can they "cut through the mustard" if the first thing we do is unload a couple hundred barrels of it at their door?

Many teams have a breakout sub-team charged with monitoring developing technology and recommending purchases. Theirs is a tough job, for they must tiptoe through a minefield of paradoxes:

- keeping up with new technology, without breaking the team budget
- having systems that are feature-rich and flexible, without being so complicated they are unlearnable
- systems that do the work the team needs done, without becoming a crutch, and without overshadowing the work.

These paradoxes can be killers. The sad truth is that, though the team technologies currently out there are often fantastic, teams are still tripping over their tools, wasting precious team time learning systems that don't do what we want them to or are too hard for everyone to master, and trying to get tools to do things that they just can't do yet.

Our advice to technology acquisition subteams is to research and purchase systems with the same spectrum of diagnostic concerns that the rest of this book addresses. A good system—whether it is a retractable ball point pen or a local area network—must demonstrably build upon and improve:

- team clarity
- team communication
- team trust

Team technologies to come

We have a dream, and it goes something like this: A team of ten members is scattered. Three are at a divisional headquarters in Chicago, doing product research together. Four more are employees of four different corporate partners—one is a distributor in Columbus, two are production subcontractors in Mexico City and the Philippines, and the fourth is a semiretired telecommuter in Ketchikan, Idaho. Rounding out the team are the professor in London who developed the idea the team has been working on, a marketing whiz in San Francisco, and the team's corporate sponsor, in Osaka, Japan.

At the corporate sites are computer networks and lots of machines. Divisional headquarters has the capability to do videoconferencing with the parent company in Japan. A couple of years ago this was a big deal—both groups had to troop down to their corporate video studio and sit in front of cameras to have their tete-a-tetes. But now they have little video eyes mounted in the corners of their Macs and PCs. The image is a little stiff, and the image flickers and flutters a bit, but they can now call one another at the drop of a hat and have a conversation with live video of each other on their computer screens.

The Mexico City and London offices can also be hooked into these calls. It is especially valuable to them to go face-to-face with team members because they have never actually met them. Though nervous at first, seeing their faces on-screen helped break the ice and after a while made the talks much more animated and interesting.

All ten members of the team have faxing capability with everyone else. They can either send a message straight from the computer, using a fax modem, or they can print a message, or photocopy a document, and send it by a regular fax machine. This is especially useful to the people in London and Japan, who are not usually conscious at the same time of day. Faxing helps them stay current with one another, within a few hours.

The fax modems are also useful in contacting on-line services. The Japan office subscribes to MCI Mail. Columbus is on America Online. Chicago and Japan are hooked up to CompuServe. The fellow in Ketchikan, way up at his cabin in the mountains, uses a little laptop computer and a cellular phone that is connected wirelessly to an Internet gateway in Coeur d'Alene. Using this motley assortment of online bulletin boards, the ten team members can send one another daily memos on problems they're facing and edited versions of one another's documents.

The team members in the big cities can take advantage of extra-wide information thoroughfares that can be shooting huge amounts of data back and forth. If they work with raw text data, they can upload and ship the entire Los Angeles phone book set in a few minutes. They can ship in other media too. They can ship an entire movie to one another through these wide-open gateways, or multimedia fax documents, with live video, animation, Post-It notes, an audio soundtrack. (They don't do all these things, but they could if they needed to.)

Maybe the team decides that there is too much delay using the Internet and other services, or that the team needs a mechanism that goes beyond mere memo capabilities or sending one another static multimedia documents. What if the team wanted to conduct actual, ongoing meetings, around the globe?

They could set their alarm clocks for a certain time, wake up, and do a conference call, by voice, and a secretary could take notes of the conversation and any decisions reached. Or they could communicate using the latest type of electronic meeting system, one which allows "meetings" to occur outside the realm of real time, that sets up voting situations, records everyone's ideas, and allows team members to prioritize and vote on a host of issues. Everyone enters information by keyboard; everyone sees everyone else's comments displayed and labeled by name, on their monitors.

Yes, the people in Asia and Europe would vote later, or earlier, than the American team. But they would have the same protections as the others—voting results would be announced only after everyone has voted.

What's remarkable to us about this scenario is not that it is a science-fiction techno-utopia achievable sometimes around the bend—a utopia that we never quite get to. It can all be done today, with existing, fairly robust communications technology. People in pretty ordinary organizations are doing this right now.

This is not to say, however, that these teams are not suffering from the same problems every other team has. Technology can only do a few things for teams. It can speed communications up, it can make communication easier, and maintain a cleaner paper trail. The team is still a team, no matter how much hardware and software it drags behind it, and prone to all the human frailties that all teams are prone to.

A computer will not impose clarity on a fuzzy notion. That is something only we can do.

Our prescription for our high-tech, far-flung, globally partnered team is that they make a point, maybe twice a year, of buying plane tickets and flying to some agreed-upon location, and get to know one another again, in the flesh.

Bring a swimsuit, and make it a vacation.

chapter 24

•

long-term team health

•

the well-tuned first-string team

And so we draw near the end of the team journey. We've identified the problems, confusions, and misconceptions that have been keeping the team from performing, and taken steps to get them working the way they should. You've kicked out the jams. Your group is a lean, mean, certified teaming machine.

But, of course, the team journey doesn't end here. Having attained a good team groove, you need to find ways to keep it there, and keep the groove from deteriorating into a rut. You want your team to stay hungry and in the chase—even if it has already experienced solid success and has been rewarded and recognized the way it deserves to be.

Sports cliché alert: As hard as it is to win once, it's tons harder to keep winning, year in and year out.

Automatic refocusing

How does a team survive success? By striving to maintain the same level of attention to its own processes that it maintained while it was first achieving success. The point of reference is continuous improvement, what the Japanese call *kaizen*—the idea that processes can be improved infinitely.

Continuous improvement is the way teams should think about how their outputs are received by external groups—end customers, internal customers, other teams, the enterprise as a whole. For internal purposes, we propose a parallel practice called continuous clarity—a never-relax attitude toward being the best team you can be.

The reason for continuous clarity: things change. The conditions that existed six months ago, as the team was enjoying obvious success, have given way to new conditions—the marketplace, the organization, or the team itself. The danger is that, as conditions change, the team slips out of congruency with itself. If team business is riding a roller coaster, then you want your team in the same train of cars, and on the same track.

Continuous clarity—bear with this Zen riddle—means you are *constantly re-clarifying the clarity you first achieved* during the team's inception. It's not enough for team members to come together and fully comprehend their goals and vision on Wednesday, February 12. They have to keep getting that fresh, clear understanding the next day, and the next, and the day after that. They need to obtain ongoing clarity on:

1. high-priority goals/objectives with associated short-term tasks

2. accountabilities (who's responsible, for what, by when)

3. barriers and strategies around the barriers

4. any interpersonal issues needing addressing

5. any needed modifications of leadership strategy

6. suggestions for improving inter/intra team communications.

Continuous clarity means continually enumerating the things that lead to team success, and asking if they are working, or if they need work. We ask if we have the resources we need. If not, how do we commandeer them? If we can't get them, how can we make do without them?

We think of the people adjuncts that are indispensable to team survival:

- **Team sponsor.** This is our team angel, the person that runs interference for us. Is he or she apprised of our current doings, our problems, our needs? What does he or she need to know to continue saving our bacon?

- **Team champions.** The individual or individuals high up in the organization whose idea we are, who helped get us going. Are channels to these persons open? Are they still our friends? What do they need to know to continue serving us? What do we need to know?
- **Facilitators.** The outside mediator, whether outside the team or outside the enterprise. This person has the objective eyes to help us see what we cannot see. Are we in touch? What does he or she think?
- **Team leaders.** Are the nominal team leaders and the de facto team leaders in synch with the team? What issues do they see coming down the pike? Are they having problems that they haven't informed the rest of the team about?

Without this continuous reclarification, the vision decays and the team, despite absolutely tip-top intentions, breaks up. Some team members may still be on the roller coaster track, but others have diverged and are happily tooling in disconnected coaster cars down Hollywood Boulevard, the Apian Way, or down some lonely dirt road way up in the high hills. And that's bad. Interesting, but bad.

Continuous clarity means that a team must adopt an ongoing diagnostic attitude about itself. Remember the grid at the beginning of the book, showing the ways that teams go bad, and proposed solutions? As a team member committed to maintaining continuous clarity on team excellence, you should have a copy of that grid more or less stapled to your mind. Because you need to be thinking all the time about the various ways in which teams get stuck—in order to prevent getting stuck, or to detect getting stuck as early as possible, so as to get quickly unstuck.

The grids on pages 214 and 215 lists the pitfalls teams are prone to, then three measures, and an action plan:

- Where We Were a Year Ago (Scale 1-7)
- Where We Are Right Now (Scale 1-7)
- Where We Want to Be a Year from Now (Scale 1-7)

When in doubt about your team's current condition of alertness, the grid can serve as a five-minute diagnostic course to identify where

Long-Term Team Health		
Problem	**Where We Were a Year Ago (Scale 1–7)**	**Where We Are Right Now (Scale 1–7)**
Mismatched Needs		
Confused Goals, Cluttered Objectives		
Unresolved Roles		
Bad Policies, Stupid Procedures		
Bad Decision Making		
Personality Conflicts		
Bad Leadership		
Bleary Vision		
Anti-Team Cluture		
Communication Shortfalls		
Ill-Conceived Reward Systems		
Lack of Team Trust		
Unwillingness to Change		
The Wrong Tools		

problems are occurring, identify where targeted goals are not being met, and move teams to plan remedies. Use this grid, or one of your own that lists problems your particular team is prone to, to maintain a diagnostic attitude that keeps your team from slipping too far from its intended path.

Long-Term Team Health (cont'd)		
Problem	**Where We Want to Be a Year from Now (Scale 1–7)**	**Action Plan Notes: What We will Do to Get There**
Mismatched Needs		
Confused Goals, Cluttered Objectives		
Unresolved Roles		
Bad Policies, Stupid Procedures		
Bad Decision Making		
Personality Conflicts		
Bad Leadership		
Bleary Vision		
Anti-Team Cluture		
Communication Shortfalls		
Ill-Conceived Reward Systems		
Lack of Team Trust		
Unwillingness to Change		
The Wrong Tools		

Diagnostic dangers

Having said what we just said, we feel the need to offer a proviso:

It is good for teams to cultivate a diagnostic attitude,
to maintain this continuous clarity.
It is bad to fall in love with the idea.

Usually there is someone on the team who has a knack for the kind of circumspect, see-around-corners thinking that ongoing diagnosis requires. This person is just wired a bit differently from most people. He or she may be a bit of a worrier but quite good at seeing the big picture and identifying minute variations of team behavior that are leading it astray.

Some teams don't have anyone matching this description. They aren't able to designate anyone as the clarity controller, and they have a dickens of a time staying focused. Other teams have the opposite problem—one or more members become infatuated with the task of diagnosis. They are indeed blessed with the ability to see where the group is slipping off the tracks, and that blessing becomes a curse. They go around all day spotting discrepancies, crying *aha!*, and generally confusing the team worse than it was confusing itself.

We call it diagnostic overload. It happens when the call to clarity itself becomes a distraction. You hear it as one of the wilder aphorisms of the TQM movement, like "If it ain't broke, break it," or "Don't put a fire out when you can prevent it in the first place."

These people are too in love with clarity. Their ego and self-esteem are too bound up in detecting minute variations. They envision the effective team as a crackling synaptic whip of self-correcting maniacs. A pleasant idea, to be sure, but the reality is that fires are a part of most of our jobs, and when we are on fire, it makes sense to put it out, not pause for a lyrical meditation on the beauty of prevention.

If you think about it, making a cult of clarification was one of the things teams were implemented to avoid. Teams, you will recall, replaced a system of multilayered controls—other people whose sole job was to keep an eye on you. Let's don't do that again.

Creating a learning organization

The point of a team today is to exploit the current knowledge and intelligence of its people. The point of a team over time is for the knowledge and intelligence to grow, cross-pollinate, and multiply. This is what learning is.

There is no color-by-numbers formula for creating a learning organization. Unfortunately, how to learn, as well as what to learn, are part of the learning process. Learning guru Peter Senge identifies five dimensions of learning that every individual, every team, and every organization can begin to master. They begin with identifying our current learning habits and traits and proceed to improve or replace them with habits and traits that open inquiry up instead of shutting it down.

☛ **Building personal mastery.** Teams are groups of individuals performing first as individuals for their own reasons. When each of us learns, we expand our ability to see, communicate, and understand. When we have the power finally to articulate what we want to be and do, our purposefulness is hard to deny—it leads naturally to an atmosphere of commitment.

☛ **Surfacing mental models.** What do we say we believe, and what do we really believe? In order to learn, our minds must first be freed of the clutter of assumptions and paradigms that bog us down repeating the same old errors. By allowing our mental models of the way things are to surface, we can finally critique them and replace them with truer models.

☛ **Building shared vision.** It is vital to move beyond "the vision thing"—the conventional team leader furnishing a vision, and everyone else marching in step. The entire team must take part in fashioning a new kind of vision, one in which we tell one another what we want to create together, as individuals and as team members. Our shared pictures of the future become our organizational vision.

☛ **Team learning.** Personal mastery is good, but team mastery is our goal. Learning alone is important—learning with other people is even more important. Our skills of talking and listening and thinking must all be ratcheted up, until a true group intelligence is created.

☛ **Systems thinking.** The "big picture," systems thinking takes us beyond absorbing raw data, beyond syllogisms, until we can see ideas as "stories"—the drama of what we know, and where we intend to go. Systems thinking means we are adults, no longer gear-twiddlers, capable of seeing how things interlock and using our intelligence and shared information to improve the system. Eventually we discern the patterns of the system we are part of and learn the language of interconnected causes and effects.

People sometimes equate information and knowledge. Deming draws an important distinction between them, and a common misconception. Information is what the world is overflowing with—data, facts, words in books, bytes saved as electronic storage. Information is good, and indispensable for the completion of many tasks.

But it is not possible to have as much information as we need—no matter if we read every book, monitor the entire Internet, and watch every channel on the tube. Eventually, we have to say, *woah*, no more, to the avalanche of information that constantly, cheerfully overwhelms us.

That is where knowledge comes in—a point of view about the information, a theory that gives it contour and bite. It happens inside us, and only inside us. It is the magical transformation that makes us human, that allows us to change. We inhale information, we exhale knowledge.

chapter 25

epilogue

Teams are surely a fad, judging by the many books and seminars out there competing for mindshare these days. And yet, it is a fateful fad. All the hoopla about it being the wave of the future is true. Individual teams may disband, or remix, or get shuffled into some new entity. But the idea of teams isn't going away, because it's simply not possible—it's simply not affordable—to return to the days of multiple supervisory levels.

Given that inevitability, shouldn't we be trying to team right?

We began this book by promising we weren't going to be another team happy-talk book. Teams are trouble, because they're made of people, and people are trouble.

The happy-talk books pretended that just murmuring the mantra of teams would cause all the creepy organizational goblins to fall away—inefficiency, low productivity, befuddled processes, high cost, bloated workforce, poor morale, poor return on investment. And the teams would magically outperform the old system, and everyone would get along, and you wouldn't need the metal detector at shareholders meetings. Quality without tears.

Ain't no such thing as quality, or any kind of continuous organizational improvement, without tears. In fact, tears—meaning, sincerity, commitment, and caring about the people you work with—are probably the proper starting point for true improvement.

We talked for so many years about "the bottom line," meaning quarterly profits, that we are having trouble today acknowledging that there are several bottom lines. Instead of just lying awake at night worrying about share price, we have to worry about:

- whether team leadership is truly leading
- whether the team understands the organizational vision, or its own goals and objectives
- whether all the knowledge and intelligence of every team member is being fully exploited
- whether the people that make up the team are getting their nonteam needs met

These are not concerns that business schools have ever claimed to teach. And yet, in the brave new world of teams that is materializing around us, they are the concerns that will keep the modern organization alive and competitive.

Team members do not have to be best friends to be a good team. Heaven knows, every team has its curmudgeons, dullards, flakes, nerds, and zealots. (When you think about it, what else is there?)

But we can know one another, and accept that that's the way we are—and learn that, just below the surface, our peculiarities fade, and we are just people, working to solve our individual problems, trying to make the best of imperfect situations. Psychoanalyst Terry Warner talks about a "principle of agency," by which all team members become agents for one another, charged with the task of making one another's dreams come true.

A better analogy than friends is family. Like members of a family, team members do not generally ask to be thrown together. Like all families, all teams are flawed. Like families, teams have their high points and their low points. Fights break out. Emotions flare.

And just as families usually pool together in crisis and set their misgivings aside, so must teams. We spend as much, or more, time with team members as we do with our real families. And the dreams of our real families often are so bound up in the aspirations of the teams we belong to.

It's all a circle—of need, desire, and ultimately of love. The really successful teams we have seen have almost all been marked by a sincere spirit of wanting the best for one another.

If the team movement arose from any single ethic it was that people are not cogs and levers, as the old organization diagrams suggested. We are human beings. So often, as teams slip into dysfunction, that is our downfall.

But when people take the time to learn about one another, what is in their hearts as well as in their minds, we rise to a higher level. Call it love, call it camaraderie, call it team spirit, or don't call it anything at all. But somehow or other, you have to get there. It is the glory of working together, and getting things right.

index

a

"The Abilene Paradox," 120
Acclimation to teams, 187, 188–91
Accomplishments, celebrating, 117
Acid River, 173
Acknowledgment
    of team members by leader, 86
    trust and, 145
Action forums, 166–67
Advantages of teams, 11–13
Adventure learning, myth of,
    171–74
Affiliation needs, 17–20
Agreement, change and, 161
Ambiguity, information
    interpretation and, 150
Amiable personality type, 54,
    55–56, 57, 58
Analytical personality type, 54, 55,
    57, 58–59
Atmosphere in teams, 107–17
Attitude, information interpretation
    and, 150–51
Authority rule
    with discussion, 44–45
    without discussion, 44
Averaging, in decision making,
    43–44
Awards, 134–35
Awareness, leaders and, 96

b

Bardwick, Judith, 67, 68
Behavior types, 54–59. See also
    Personality type, myth of
    amiables, 54, 55–56, 57, 58
    analyticals, 54, 55, 57, 58–59
    drivers, 54, 55, 56, 57–58
    expressives, 54, 55, 56, 57, 58
Blame
    of team members by leader,
        87–88
    trust and, 144–45
Business history, 9–10

c

Careers of team members, leaders
    oblivious to, 90
Cash compensation, 132–33
Change, 153–67
    adaptation difficulties
        people and, 157–58
        process and, 158–59
        structure and, 159
    leaders and, 95
    leveraging, 166–67
    resistance, 157–58
    rules for teams, 159–60
        agreement and commitment,
            161
        communication, 161–62

dealing with mistakes, 164–65
expectations of outcomes,
  162–63
follow-through and follow-up,
  164
influence/support networks,
  163
leadership, 165–66
momentum, 164
planning, 160–61
reinforcement, 165
resources, 163–64
simple techniques, 165
truths about people and, 154–57
understanding, 153–54
Choice, leaders and, 96
Clarity, continuous, 212–15
Closed-minded leaders, 82–83
Closure, for information
organization, 149
Collaboration, 108
Commitment, change and, 161
Communication, 119–28. See also
Developmental stages of teams
change and, 155, 158, 161–62
feedback, 125–28
horror stories, 120–21
by leaders, 84, 94, 98–99
learning to listen, 122–25
misunderstandings, 52–53, 149
sensitivity and trust, 145–46
shortfalls, 119–28
technology and, 202–10
of vision, pitfalls in, 104–6
Compensation, financial, 132–33
Competition in teams, 107–9
Computer technology, 18, 202–6
Concept of teams, 7–16
Conflict
leaders and, 90–91
between teams, 31–32
within teams, 21–24, 39–40,
  51–71
  confronting, 115
  storming stage, 191–97
Consensus decision making, 42

Consideration
in leaders, 82, 84–85
in team members, 115, 145–46
Consultants, 112–14
Control, rigid, 41
Cooperation, leaders influencing,
  98–99
Core team members, 110
Corporate orientations, 13–15
Covey, Stephen, 140
Creativity, leaders supporting, 99
Credit, trust and, 145
Criticism, 127. See also Feedback

d

Danger in the Comfort Zone, 67
Decision making
bad, 41–42
inclusive, 116
methods
  authority rule with discussion,
    44–45
  authority rule without
    discussion, 44
  averaging, 43–44
  consensus, 42
  majority, 42–43
  minority, 43
trust and, 143–44
Definition of team, 10
Deming, Wm. Edwards, 11, 30, 85,
  136, 218
Denominator companies, 14–15
Developmental stages of teams
forming, 188–91
norming, 197–98
performing, 198–200
storming, 191–97
Diagnosis, ongoing, 214–16
Difficult people
blowhards, 63–66
brats, 67–69
dark angels, 69–71
jerks, 60–63
Diversity

leaders and, 91–92
in teams, 201–2
Driver personality type, 54, 55, 56, 57–58
The Druid's Knot, 172

e

Einstein, Albert, 145
Electronic meeting systems, 203
E-mail, 203, 206
Employee ownership, 133
Empowerment of team members
by leaders, 95
trust and, 147
Energy, leaders and, 94, 98
Entitlement attitude, 67
Ethics of leaders, 88–89
Evaluation
continuous, 211–16
grid for, 215–16
Expectations
for change, 162–63
perceptions and, 148
Expressive personality type, 54, 55, 56, 57, 58
Extroverts, 176

f

Facilitators, 213
Failure
intolerance by leaders, 86–87
positive approach to, 165
Fairness, trust and, 142–43
Favoritism of leaders, 86
Faxes, 208
Fear, change and, 158
Federal Aviation Authority, 121
Feedback, 116, 125–28
Feeling orientation, 176
Figure-ground, 148–49
Focus, leaders and, 97
Follow-through and follow-up,
change and, 159, 164
Ford Taurus, 49–50

Forming, as team developmental stage, 187, 188–91

g

Gainsharing, 132–33
General Motors, 10, 184
Saturn, 49–50
Goals, 29–36. See also Vision
commitment to, 115
conflicts and, 31–32
good team, 31
long-term vs. short-term, 33–35
passion and, 36
personal vs. team, 21–24
socialwork, 25–26
stretch, 32–33
trust and, 141–42
Goal sludge, 35–36
Groupware, 202–4
Growth orientation, 14, 16

h

Hamel, Gary, 13
Harvey, Jerry B., 120
Heskett, James, 88
Hidden agendas, 23
History of organizations and
management, 8–10
Honeywell, 109
Human needs, 17–24
Human problems, 51–71
Hurst, Sue Miller, 123

i

IBM, 9, 184
Ideas, free contribution of, 116
Ignorance, in leaders, 81
Improvement
continuous, 212
leaders and, 100–101
Inconsistent leaders, 85
Individual differences, 116
Individual vs. team needs, 21–24
Industrial Age, 8–9

Influence networks, change and, 163

Information
   interpretation, 150–52
   knowledge vs., 218
   organization, 148–50
   selective perception, 148
Initiative of leaders, 99–100
Innovation, leaders and, 99
Integration, leaders and, 97
Intelligence, lack of, in leaders, 80
Interpretation of information, 150–52
Intimacy, performing and, 199
Introverts, 176
Intuitive personality, 176
Involvement
   change and, 161
   of leaders, 94–95
Isolation as punishment, 18, 19

j

James, Jennifer, 91
Japan, development since World War II, 11
Job descriptions, 37
Jung, C. G., 175, 176
Juran, Joseph, 87

k

Knowledge, information vs., 218
Koch, Ed, 125

l

Laziness, change and, 158
Leaders/leadership, 75–101
   change and, 165–66
   hard charger and quiet warrior, 76–78
   myths, 78–79
   poor, changing, 80
   positive activities of, 92–101
   problems of, 80–92
   selection of, 78

spectrum of, 79
   in storming stage, 192, 194–95
   value added by, 93
   vision of, goals and, 30
Learning, 119–20
   adventure, myth of, 171–74
   how to listen, 122–25
   leaders influencing, 97
Learning organization, creating, 216–18
Leskin, Barry, 129
Lies. See Trust
Listening
   empathic, 116
   learning, 122–25
   trust and, 142–43
Long-term goals, 33–34
Lotus Notes, 204
Loyalty, trust and, 144

m

Machine age, 9
Mack, Connie, 89
Majority decision making, 42–43
Managers. See Leaders/leadership
Manuals, policies and procedures, 47–50
MBTI, 53–54, 175, 177
Melrose, Ken, 90
Mental models, 217
Merril, David, 54
Minority decision making, 43
Mistakes, change and, 164–65
Misunderstandings, 52–53, 149
Mobs, teams vs., 110–12
Momentum, change and, 156, 158, 164
Monitoring of teams, 127–28
Motorola, 32
Myers-Briggs Type Inventory, 53–54, 175, 177
Myths, 171–84
   adventure learning, 171–74
   leadership, 78–79

people liking working together, 179–80
personality type, 175–77
productivity of teamwork, 181–82
size of teams, 183–84

n

Napoleon, 42
National Reconnaissance Office, 121
Needs
individual vs. team, 21–24
perceptions and, 148
social, 17–20
Negativity, leaders and, 100
Networking technology, 203–4
Networks, influence/support, change and, 163
New members integrated into teams, 195–96
Norming, as team developmental stage, 187, 197–98
Numerator companies, 14–15

o

Objectives. See also Goals
confused, 29–36
Openness, trust and, 142–43
Opinion-makers, change and, 163
Opinions, respecting, trust and, 146–47
Organizational karma, 115
Organizational Dynamics, 120
Organization of information, 148–50
Organizations
evolution, 9–10
learning, 216–18
Orientation, information interpretation and, 151

p

Participation, change and, 161
Passion, in goal-setting, 36

Passive leaders, 92
Pathway, change and, 166
Peck, Scott, 70
People in teams, 51–71
change and, 154–58
People liking working together, myth of, 179–80
Perception
personality and, 176
trust and, 147–52
Performance
feedback, 116
leaders and, 99
Performing, as team developmental stage, 187, 198–200
Perseverance by leaders, 95–96
Personal computers, 202–6
Personalities in teams, 51–71
difficult people, 59–71
myth of personality type, 175–77
types, 53–59
Personal mastery, building, 217
Personal vs. team needs, 21–24
Perspective of leaders, 96–97
Persuasion by leaders, 95–96
Pilot projects, 167
Planning for change, 160–61
Play, work vs., 26
Policies and procedures manuals, 47–50
Positive atmosphere, creating, 114–17
Positive reinforcement, change and, 165
Positivism of leaders, 100
Procedures (and policies) manuals, 47–50
Processes, change and, 158–59
Productivity of teamwork vs. individual work, myth of, 181–82
Profit sharing, 133
Protection of team members by leader, 87–88
Psychological context, information interpretation and, 151–52

q

Quality circles at Honeywell, 109

r

Rationale for teams, 11–13
Recognition. See also Rewards and
    recognition
    methods, 132–36
    trust and, 145
Reevaluation, 211–16
Reinforcement, change and, 165
Remoteness of leaders, 89
Resistance to change, 157–58
Resources, change and, 156,
    163–64
Resource team members, 110, 112
Respecting opinions, trust and,
    146–47
Responsibility, trust and, 144–45
Rewards and recognition, 129–37
    cash compensation, 132–33
    change and, 158
    decisions about, 136–37
    ill-conceived, 129–30
    low-cost or no-cost, 134–36
    reengineered, 133–34
    security and, 131–32
    team-defined, 134
    value to team members, 132
Risks
    in adventure learning, 172
    avoidance by leaders, 90
Role acceptance in teams, 197
Roles, unresolved, 37–40

s

Sadistic approach to teams, 32–33
Sasser, Earl, 88
Saturn (automobile), 49–50
SBUs, 183
Scenarios for change, 167
Scientific management, 9
Security
    importance of, 131–32

technology and, 205
Self-serving leaders, 83
Senge, Peter, 217
Sensing personality, 176
Sensitivity, trust and, 145–46
Shewhart, Walter, 85
Short-term goals, 34–35
Size of teams, 183–84
Socialization, computer technology
    and, 18
Social needs, 17–20
Socialwork, teamwork vs., 25–26
The Spider's Web, 173
Stages toward success. See
    Developmental stages of teams
Storming, as team developmental
    stage, 187, 191–97
Strategic business units, 183
Stretch goals, 32–33
Structures, change and, 159
Styles of leadership, ineffective,
    83–84
Success
    continuing, 211–16
    opportunities, leaders and, 97
    stages (see Developmental stages
        of teams)
Suggestions in teams, 205
Support networks, change and, 163
Support of team members, trust
    and, 144
Suspicion. See Trust
Systems thinking, 217–18

t

Talent, excessive, of leaders, 82
Talking, listening and, 123–24
Tasks
    linkage, leaders and, 97
    undesirable, 38–40
Taurus (automobile), 49–50
Taylor, Frederick, 9
Teaching, 97, 119–20
Teams

adjuncts and resource personnel, 184, 212–13
concept of, 7–16
connotations of term, 8
deciding on need for, 114
definition, 10
developmental stages, 187–200
ideal vs. real, 51
long-term health of, 211–18
myths, 171–84
problems, symptoms, and solutions, 14–15, 107–17
rationale and advantages, 11–13
structure, leadership and, 79
types, 7
Teamwork, socialwork vs., 25–26
Technology, 201–10
effectiveness of, 204–6
future, 208–10
groupware, 202–4
plunging into, 206–7
Telecommuting, 206
Termination, 64
Thinking
orientation, in personality, 176
systems thinking, 217–18
Training
excessive, for leaders, 82
technology and, 205
Trust, 139–52
perceptions and, 147–52
strategies for creating, 141–47
Trust Falls, 172
Tuckman, B. W., 187
Turf Wars, 139
Turf wars, 39–40
Typology, 175–76
Tyranny in teams, 109–10

u

Unethical leaders, 88–89
Univac, 9
U.S. Navy, 122
U.S. Steel, 10

v

Vision
building shared, 217
change and, 166
of leaders, goals and, 30
nature of, 103–4
pitfalls in communicating, 104–6

w

Wants, perceptions and, 148
Warner, Terry, 220
What-if scenarios, 167
Will to team, 71
Work, play vs., 26
Workaholics, 198–99

Ever Onward

The book is over but the pain goes on.

We would like very much to hear your team experiences — what problems you ran into, what solutions you came up with. Call, fax, or write us at:

Robbins & Robbins

2475 Ridgewater Dr.
Minnetonka, MN 55305
612-544-9260 voice & FAX
email: robbi004@maroon.tc.umn.edu